10p.

DIVORCE

THE THINGS YOU THOUGHT YOU'D NEVER NEED TO KNOW

by

JILL M. BLACK,
B.A. Dunelm
of the Inner Temple and the
North Eastern Circuit, Barrister

PAPERFRONTS

ELLIOT RIGHT WAY BOOKS, KINGSWOOD, SURREY, U.K.

Made and Printed in Great Britain by Robert Hartnoll (1985) Ltd, Bodmin, Cornwall

CONTENTS

NOTE: This book deals with the law in force in England and Wales only. Whilst the legal position in relation to divorces in Scotland and Northern Ireland may be similar to that described here in many respects, there are also important differences.

If your divorce will be dealt with in Scotland or Northern Ireland, you are advised to refer to a publication that deals specifically with the law of the country concerned, or to consult a solicitor in the appropriate country.

PART 1: GENERAL INFORMATION AND FIRST CONSIDERATIONS

1
About this Book

It is so easy to look upon divorce as someone else's problem – something that will never happen to you. Most people are prepared to offer sympathy and good advice to friends and relations who are going through the process of separation and divorce. But, if your own marriage starts to break down, it comes as a shock and as you embark on the business of getting divorced you may feel anxious, helpless and very lonely. To be faced at such a time with unfamiliar and sometimes complicated legal procedures can be very daunting.

Most people appreciate the support and guidance of a solicitor at all stages of their divorce, and for some matters you really cannot do without the advice of a solicitor. This book is designed primarily for those who are consulting a solicitor but who would like to read, at their leisure, about what is involved in the process of getting divorced and how it is likely to affect them. It does not therefore give you instructions for a do-it-yourself divorce. If you are contemplating dealing with everything yourself, you should still find this book interesting and instructive reading but you will need to refer to other publications (see page 184) for further details of the procedure involved.

Getting divorced almost always involves a great deal more than simply obtaining the decree of the court that ends your marriage. You will have to cope with all sorts of problems over your property, about the children, over money etc. This book will give you an overall picture of the way in which the divorce itself is obtained and of how the more usual other problems that arise when a family breaks up are resolved. The more you understand about what is happening, the more confident you should feel about the situation. Not only will you be able to make your solicitor's job easier because you will have a good idea of the sort of information that he requires from you and of the problems that he may be encountering in helping you to sort out your affairs, but you will also be sure that you are not missing out on help from your solicitor or the courts, simply because you did not know that it was available.

Divorce law has grown up slowly through legislation made by Parliament and through cases decided by the courts. A lot of the law is complex and detailed and it would be impossible to go into it all in a book this size. One of the problems of a book on divorce is that divorce is never the same for any two families because, of course, each family has its own individual problems. Nevertheless, the basic legal procedures do not differ from case to case and a lot of the difficulties associated with a divorce crop up time and again. This book does not attempt to cover unusual points that may arise in a few divorces nor can it give personal advice to each reader – this is where a solicitor can be particularly helpful. It simply aims to help you to cope with most of the problems that you will encounter in the course of your divorce and to provide you with sufficient information to replace the myths and rumours that circulate about divorce with a basic knowledge of the law as it is likely to affect you.

2
An Introduction to Divorce

As far as possible this book steers clear of technical legal terms. Those used can be readily understood by anyone, even if he has no knowledge of the law. Nevertheless, getting divorced is a legal procedure and you are bound to hear lawyers and court officials using unfamiliar terms. Legal procedures and documents are given titles as a convenient shorthand method of referring to them, for example, you may already have made a 'will' stating to whom you want your property to pass when you die, and you will no doubt understand what is meant by 'conveying' a house.

Where technical terms are used in this book, you will generally find them explained when they are first mentioned. However, there are several words that you need to understand at the outset. The purpose of this chapter is to explain them and to give you a bird's eye view of the whole process of getting a divorce – once you have absorbed these basic terms there should be no difficulty in understanding the rest of the book.

The bare bones of the divorce procedure

The formal procedure for obtaining a divorce begins when one spouse decides that the marriage is at an end and presents the divorce court with a formal document known as the *divorce petition* asking for the marriage to be terminated. This book has been written on the basis that it is the wife who will be seeking the divorce – this is for the sake of simplicity only and the choice of the wife rather than the husband is entirely arbitrary. In fact, both husband and wife have exactly the same rights to seek a divorce and you can take it that anything which is said in relation to a wife in the following chapters will also apply to the husband and vice versa, unless the contrary is expressly stated.

Once the divorce procedure is under way, the spouse who presented the petition will be known as the *petitioner* and the other spouse will be known as the *respondent*.

A step by step outline of the course of divorce proceedings follows below. The proceedings do not actually affect the marriage in any way until the court pronounces a *decree nisi* of divorce. This is a provisional court order indicating that, provided there are no unforeseen hitches (such as problems over the arrangements that have been made for the children) the court will be prepared to grant a final divorce in a few weeks. The divorce becomes permanent and fully effective only when this final order is made – it is called the *decree absolute* of divorce. Not until this stage is reached is either spouse free to remarry.

When one spouse seeks a divorce because of adultery of the other spouse, and names the other person involved in the adultery in the divorce petition, that person is entitled to have his or her say in the divorce proceedings and is known as the *co-respondent*.

The procedure step by step

1. The petitioner consults a solicitor about divorce (or, if she intends to deal with the divorce herself, goes to the County

Court office to obtain the necessary forms and an explanatory booklet about divorce procedure).

2. The divorce papers are prepared (for example, the divorce petition and a statement as to the arrangements that are being made for the children after the divorce).

3. The divorce papers are 'filed' (or formally presented) at the court office by the petitioner or her solicitor. The divorce proceedings are now under way.

4. If either spouse is in immediate financial difficulty, he or she can ask the court to make a temporary maintenance order for him or herself or to deal with the question of maintenance for the children.

5. The court sends the respondent (and the co-respondent if there is one) copies of the divorce papers and instructions on what he should do about the divorce.

6. The respondent (and co-respondent) decide(s) whether he wants to seek advice from a solicitor and consults one, at once, if he decides he does.

7. The respondent (and co-respondent) decide(s) whether he wishes to object to the divorce being granted.

8. The respondent (and co-respondent) or his solicitor complete(s) the form known as the acknowledgement of service which he will have received from the court with the divorce papers, showing that he has received all the documents and indicating what he proposes to do about the divorce. He should do this within eight days of receiving the papers in the first place.

9. In most cases the respondent (and co-respondent) will indicate that they do not wish to oppose the divorce. The court will then notify the petitioner that she can proceed with the case.

10. The petitioner or her solicitor completes a form known as an affidavit of evidence, confirming that what she said in her petition is correct. She will be required to swear on the Bible that this is so in the presence of another solicitor.

11. The petitioner or her solicitor delivers the affidavit of evidence to the court office and asks the court to give directions about the granting of the divorce decree.

12. The Registrar (a very senior court official) considers the case privately. If he is satisfied that the petitioner is entitled to a divorce, he fixes the day on which this will be pronounced by the Judge. If there are children, he will also fix an appointment for the petitioner (and/or the respondent) to meet the Judge to go over the arrangements for them.

13. Provided the Registrar is satisfied that everything is in order, the court will inform the petitioner and the respondent (and the co-respondent) when the divorce decree will be pronounced and when the Judge will consider the arrangements for the children.

14. The Judge pronounces decree nisi of divorce in court. Either party can attend if they wish, but neither is obliged to do so.

15. The court is now able to consider long term financial arrangements – when it actually does so will depend on all the circumstances of the particular case.

16. The petitioner and/or the respondent attends the appointment with the Judge to discuss the arrangements for the children.

17. Provided that the Judge is satisfied with the arrangements for the children, the petitioner has only to wait for six weeks to elapse from the date on which decree nisi was pronounced before she can apply for the final divorce decree, decree absolute. This application will be made by her or her solicitor at the court office.

18. Decree absolute is granted. The court sends a certificate of decree absolute to the petitioner and the respondent. The divorce is now complete and both spouses are now free to remarry. There may, however, be outstanding questions over custody and access in relation to the children, or over property or maintenance. These will be cleared up as soon as possible.

You will notice that no mention has been made of the earliest time when the court will consider questions of custody of the children and access to them nor of personal protection of one of the spouses or of the children from the other spouse. This is because with such serious matters it is always possible to obtain help from the court, if necessary even before divorce proceedings have been commenced.

One lady's experience of divorce

Mrs. Jones's case is fairly typical of a straightforward divorce and will give you an idea of what to expect. She had been married for over twenty years – the earlier part of the marriage had been quite happy, but in the last five years her relationship with her husband had got progressively worse. It started with arguments over trivial things, which began to get more frequent and more heated. Her husband was not giving her enough money on which to manage and was spending a great deal of his time and his money at the local pub. He began to be abusive towards her and to run her down in front of friends. Eventually the arguments became so bad that Mr. Jones would be violent towards Mrs. Jones, slapping her and sometimes even punching her about her face and body. Now that there was only one child left at home, Carol who was then fourteen (all the others had grown up and got married) she decided that she could not take any more and that she would try to get a divorce.

She went to see a solicitor who was recommended to her by a friend. He spent some time discussing things with her and explaining what was involved in a divorce. He was able to tell her that because she had very little income and capital, she would be able to benefit from legal aid (see page 22 onwards) which would take care of most of her legal costs at least until her financial affairs were sorted out with her husband. This was a relief to her as she found that, for the immediate future, she would only have to pay a modest sum for her solicitor's assistance. The solicitor prepared the documents necessary for the divorce proceedings from the information that she gave him. These included the divorce petition (which set out details of her marriage to her husband and her complaints about his behaviour) and a document detailing the arrangements she proposed for Carol after the divorce. The documents were presented at the court and the court arranged for copies to be sent to her husband. He decided that he would not raise any objections to the divorce and sent the acknowledgement of service form back to the court informing them of his decision.

He decided to move out of the house and was lucky enough to find a flat to rent quite reasonably. Mrs. Jones's solicitor prepared an affidavit of evidence for her, confirming in writing everything she had said in her petition and took her to the office of another solicitor where she read through the affidavit and took an oath swearing that the affidavit was correct. When the affidavit was delivered to the court, the court was able to pass the papers on to the Registrar who was satisfied that there should be a divorce. The Judge pronounced decree nisi of divorce – although this was done in a public court, Mrs. Jones did not attend as she preferred not to do so.

However, she did have to go to court for the interview that had been fixed for her with the Judge to discuss the arrangements for Carol. There was no problem about this because Mr. Jones had always agreed that Carol should go on living with her mother and that they should both be able to live in the family home. The Judge said he was quite sure that Carol would be properly looked after and also made a custody order in favour of Mrs. Jones and an order that Mr. Jones should be able to have reasonable access. Six weeks after decree nisi was granted Mrs. Jones's solicitor helped her to go ahead and obtain decree absolute of divorce. He told her that she was then free to remarry if she wished, as could Mr. Jones.

There was still the family property to be sorted out, particularly the house, because, although Mr. Jones wanted Mrs. Jones and Carol to go on living there, he was insisting that this should only go on until Carol was 18 and that the house should then be sold. Some arrangement had also to be made over maintenance, although this was not too much of a problem as Mrs. Jones had got a job soon after her husband had left home. Because Mr. and Mrs. Jones were not able to agree over what should be done, some time after the divorce came through the court considered the whole matter and decided for them. Mrs. Jones and Carol were permitted to go on living in the family home for as long as they wanted although when it was sold Mr. Jones was to get a share in the proceeds. Mr. Jones would get the car and the caravan and some savings that they had in the building society. With this behind him, he thought he should be able to buy his own place with the help of a mortgage. Because Mrs. Jones had got a job, she did not need any maintenance for herself, but the court decided that Mr. Jones should pay maintenance each week for Carol.

Mr. and Mrs. Jones no longer see each other now. Mrs. Jones went through a very bad patch after the divorce when she felt depressed and dissatisfied with life, but she got over that in time and has made a fresh start. She now has a very enjoyable social life but is not thinking of remarrying, at least for some time. Carol still sees her father regularly, almost every week. They never made any fixed arrangements about when they should see each other because Mr. Jones shortly after the divorce obtained his own small house which was on Carol's way home from school. She is able to call in as and when she wants. On occasions, she has stayed overnight when her mother has been away. Although Mr. Jones misses his wife and daughter a great deal, he has begun to face up to the fact that divorce was probably the best solution for the family.

Judicial separation and nullity

You may have heard of two other court orders that can affect a marriage – a decree of *nullity* and a decree of *judicial separation.* Neither of these is very common these days.

A decree of nullity is used to terminate a marriage instead of a decree of divorce when for some reason the marriage has never been properly valid. This can happen if, for example, the marriage has never been consummated by sexual intercourse because one spouse has refused to have sexual intercourse or has been unable to do so or where the marriage was never a proper marriage because the spouses were too closely related to each other. Once a decree of nullity has been pronounced, both spouses are free to remarry just as they are after a divorce.

If it turns out that a nullity decree would be more appropriate than a divorce in your case, your solicitor will tell you and will see that all the necessary steps are taken for you. Although the procedure will be similar in some respects to the procedure for getting a divorce, there will be differences, for example, you will have to attend a court hearing when the Judge will determine whether you should be granted a decree of nullity or not. The court will be able to resolve questions of finance and property, difficulties over the children etc. just as it can when it grants a divorce.

A decree of judicial separation does not actually end the marriage and neither spouse is free to remarry after it. What it does do is to give the court's formal seal of approval to the spouses' living apart. The court can resolve all the problems that are likely to attend the separation (over property, children etc.) just as it can when it grants a divorce. The procedure for obtaining a judicial separation is almost identical to that for obtaining a divorce, except that there is only one decree of judicial separation whereas there are two divorce decrees, a preliminary one and a final one (see also page 16).

3
Making Sure You Are Doing The Right Thing

Is divorce what you really want?

Strange though it may seem, these days divorce is far more final than getting married – it will put an end to your marriage for ever. Once the final divorce decree is granted the only way in which you will be able to change your mind will be to get married to your former spouse all over again, always assuming that he or she is willing to do so after what you have both been through.

So it is as well to pause before plunging into divorce proceedings to make sure that you really do want to be divorced. Look through the rest of this book so that you are certain of what a divorce involves. Ask yourself truthfully what your motives are. Do you want a divorce because you honestly feel that your marriage is at an end and there is no chance that you will ever get back together again? If so, then no doubt divorce is the best course for you. But you may find that you really do not intend to go through with the divorce proceedings at all – perhaps you are hoping that by taking the step of claiming the divorce you will make your partner realise just how close he or she has come to losing you and how much it would hurt if he or she did? Maybe you are trying to wound your partner in retaliation for something he or she has done that has caused you pain? If you suspect that you may be using the divorce proceedings in this way, stop and think again. Asking for a divorce is unlikely to be successful as a device to bring your spouse back to you and it may well make things considerably worse between you by causing him or her to feel resentful and angry towards you. What is more, although at the outset you do not intend to go the whole hog and get divorced, once you have set the wheels in motion you may find that they are very difficult to stop and that you are, in fact, divorced almost before you know it.

What are the alternatives?

It is all very well to say 'Don't get a divorce', but what else can you do if your marriage is in serious difficulties? In fact there are a number of alternatives.

Perhaps the first to consider is the possibility of sorting everything out and making your marriage a success again. This will probably entail talking your problems and complaints over at length with your spouse. You may also want to seek assistance from an independent person who can help you to make the first moves towards a reconciliation and give you some general guidance. There are a number of organisations who are prepared to do this: perhaps one of the most famous is the Marriage Guidance Council – you will find a few more details of their work and how to contact them in Chapter 27.

You may also be able to obtain legal help from the courts of a less radical nature than a divorce. For example, your solicitor will be able to advise you about the courts' powers to sort out particular problems that may have arisen, for instance over money or the children or the occupation of the house, without actually going to the lengths of granting you a divorce. Another alternative that might appeal to those who have objections to a divorce, perhaps on religious grounds, but who still wish to sever all connections with their spouse, is a judicial separation. This puts your separation on a formal basis and enables the court to sort out questions of maintenance and property for you without actually ending your marriage. Or you may wish to consider entering into a separation agreement with your spouse in which you can make arrangements for living apart from each other without getting divorced, or going to court at all.

How do you sort out what you do want?
It is not always easy to step back and take a cool look at your own situation and you may want to talk things over with someone to get your ideas straight. Whom can you turn to?

Your problems over your marriage are probably all you can think about and it would be very easy to feel you were becoming a nuisance to friends and relations by constantly unburdening yourself to them. Obviously, you cannot expect them to listen to your problems day in and day out, but they will almost certainly be prepared to talk over your troubles at least once if you think it might help to share them. Even if they cannot offer you advice, you may find that your feelings are clearer and you are calmer because you have talked about everything. However, you will have to be very careful not to make your listener feel uncomfortable by trying to get him or her 'on your side'. Most people are unwilling to be drawn into someone else's private life (even if that someone else is a relation) and you will soon find that you have difficulty persuading anyone to listen to you if you adopt this kind of attitude. Furthermore, if friends and relations do become directly involved, this is likely to make things much more difficult for you with your spouse, as feelings may well become inflamed on both sides.

If you do not want to share your troubles with friends and relations, you can always turn to organisations such as the Marriage Guidance Council as mentioned above – they are not solely concerned with getting couples back together again and will be quite prepared even when that is not possible to help you to sort out your own wishes for the future

Do not overlook your solicitor in these early stages. He probably will not have time to listen to all your problems, nor is he qualified to help with reconciliation etc. himself, but there is a lot he can do and there is no need to wait until you have decided on divorce before you go to see him. If you go at a time when you have still not made up your mind, he will be able to make sure that you understand all that a divorce would involve and will tell you about any alternatives that may be suitable in your case. He may also be able to refer you to local organisations who could help you.

There are other people who may be able to assist you if you have any special problems, for example your general practitioner if your health is suffering as a result of the difficulties with your marriage, or in emotional turmoil perhaps your clergyman. A few people suffer undue despair or even feel suicidal temporarily. The Samaritans in the local phone book volunteer round the clock help with such feelings.

Remember that it is usually unfair to involve your children in your deliberations. They are probably able to sense that things are going wrong in the marriage and they are likely to be very distressed that their parents are not happy. It is not going to help them if they have to share your worries with you as well and they will probably resent being drawn onto one side or the other. It will be the responsibility of you and your spouse to see that you explain everything to them in as rational and unbiased a way as possible and prepare them as best you can for your separation or divorce if you decide that this is inevitable.

Not looking back once the divorce is over

Once your divorce comes through, you will probably feel very lonely for some time. You will have to get used to being single all over again and to the problems that that can bring. These can range from the embarassment of having no partner to take to a dance or a dinner party perhaps to the loneliness of holidays on your own and some weekends when you see no one from Friday night to Monday morning.

There is no doubt that you will find adjusting to your new life hard. But it will be up to you to adopt a positive attitude to life and to set things in motion to minimise the difficulties. When you become the initiator for a few social activities, be it playing bridge or a treasure hunt for the children, it's surprising how people also put themselves out for you. Try to look upon your divorce as a fresh start. Don't wait for things to happen to brighten up your outlook – go out and make them happen. Keep in touch with people you knew whilst you were married. You will also find that there are very many other people in exactly the same position as you, either because of the death of their partner or because they too have been divorced. If you want to do so, you can probably get in touch with them through local organisations – if you don't know of any, your nearest Citizens' Advice Bureau can almost certainly come up with some addresses.

You could also consider joining societies or classes concerned with particular interests. Above all, don't keep looking back and having regrets for the way things might have been – look forward and assure yourself that you will eventually be able to make yourself a new life, however small the prospect seems at the outset.

4

Should You Consult a Solicitor? The Pros, the Cons and the Cost

There is no compulsion on you to consult a solicitor at any stage of your divorce if you do not want to do so. However as a general rule it makes good sense to take legal advice about a divorce. Exactly how much help you will require from a solicitor will depend on your own personal preference and the circumstances of your case.

Most divorces involve two stages – the initial step of obtaining the divorce decree (referred to in this chapter as 'the divorce') and the (often much more tricky) problem of making arrangements about the children, family property, maintenance etc. for the future (referred to in this chapter as 'future arrangements').

1. How can a solicitor help?

a) WITH THE DIVORCE

Fairly recently the procedure for obtaining a divorce has been simplified so that, in most cases, there is no formal court hearing and most of the divorce can be dealt with by means of paperwork. This has been done with the aim of reducing the amount of legal help required by people getting divorced and, provided the circumstances of the case are fairly straightforward, it is now possible to get divorced without ever seeing a solicitor at all.

How do you know if your case is sufficiently straightforward to handle yourself? There is no simple answer to this. It all depends on your personal circumstances and it is unfortunately not impossible for a case that seems clear cut and without problems at the outset to turn into a nightmare (and, of course, vice versa).

As a guide, as a petitioner you are most likely to be able to handle your own divorce where:

(i) your spouse is quite happy to be divorced and will not be raising any objections to your divorce petition

and (ii) you will be basing your divorce petition on the fact that your spouse has committed *adultery* (which he or she is prepared to admit to the court) or on the fact that you have been *separated for two years and your spouse consents* to the divorce or on the fact that you have been *separated for five years* (see Chapter 7 for details of the grounds for divorce).

You may also feel sufficiently confident to look after the case yourself where your spouse is content to be divorced and you intend to base your petition on his or her *behaviour* which you are quite sure is so serious that you cannot be expected to go on living with him or her.

As a respondent, you may find it possible to handle the divorce yourself provided you do not wish to object to the divorce being granted or to anything that your spouse has said about you in the petition and you are certain that you understand fully what the divorce will mean to you.

Anyone who does not fall within these categories will find the help of a solicitor invaluable.

Whilst it may be possible for you to manage without a solicitor, many people feel more comfortable if they do have legal advice. Furthermore, conducting your own divorce proceedings can turn out to be time consuming, and some people simply cannot spare the time to deal with everything themselves. As a result, a large proportion of couples going through a divorce are still seeking help from solicitors and there is absolutely no reason to feel you are being extravagant or timid if you decide to do the same.

If you do consult a solicitor, he will take charge of the divorce proceedings for you from obtaining the information that is needed to start the case off to obtaining the final decree of divorce. Although he will almost certainly complete the necessary forms for you, you will still be required to check that they are correct and, from time to time, to sign documents and possibly to deliver them to the court. He will also make sure that, if there is anything the law can do to help you, you do not have to struggle with money problems or difficulties over children, accommodation, the behaviour of your spouse etc. whilst you are waiting for the divorce to come through. The one thing you will normally still have to cope with on your own is your appointment to see the Judge about the arrangements for the children. However, this is not likely to cause you any problems as it is very informal.

As you will see from the following section, you will probably want to consult a solicitor about your future arrangements. One of the advantages of seeing a solicitor about the divorce itself is that he can also get the ball rolling in relation to future arrangements at a very early stage. This should mean that everything can be finalised by agreement between you or by the court with the minimum delay so that you can put your marriage behind you and make a fresh start as soon as possible.

b) WITH FUTURE ARRANGEMENTS

In almost every case, it is prudent (if not essential) to consult a solicitor about your future arrangements.

Some couples are fortunate enough to be able to discuss arrangements for everything with each other amicably. If you are in this position, your solicitor will ensure that the terms you have come to are the best for both of you in the long run, and will help you to record your agreements in a form that will secure the maximum tax advantage for both of you (if financial arrangements are involved) and that will lead to the least dispute in the future over exactly what was agreed.

If you find that you and your spouse get at each other's throats whenever you try to discuss things, your solicitor can fulfil a valuable role as negotiator for you. He will also advise you what you can reasonably expect by way of capital and maintenance and what you can reasonably be required to provide for your spouse. He will help you to decide what arrangements will be best, for example in relation to the children. With assistance of this kind, you will often find that it is possible to come to a solution that suits both of you without involving the court to decide for you.

If it does become necessary to ask the court to determine your future arrangements for you, your solicitor will take complete charge of the proceedings and, if a court hearing is involved, he will see that all the evidence that supports your case is put before the court and that you are represented during the hearing by either himself or a barrister.

2. Choosing a solicitor

If you have regularly consulted a solicitor in the past, you will probably want to let him deal with the divorce for you. Not all solicitors deal with matrimonial work, however, nor do they all operate under the Legal Aid and Green Form schemes which provide for subsidised legal advice (see below). If you require help of a type that your existing solicitor cannot give you, he will tell you and he may be able to pass you on to another member of his firm or suggest other firms that you could consult.

It is almost always advisable for you and your spouse to consult different solicitors over the divorce and future arrangements. If you have both consulted the same solicitor in the past, you may be reluctant to change now. If so, ask your solicitor what his view is about representing both of you. He may feel that, in your particular case, he can properly do this. On the other hand, if he feels that you should have separate solicitors, you will have to decide which of you is to seek help elsewhere. You can certainly ask your solicitor to guide you by giving you the names of some other firms who may deal with your case:

If you do not already have a solicitor, it can be a daunting task trying to choose one. A walk round any town will almost certainly reveal the nameplates of a number of firms. If you would like to see a fairly comprehensive list of the firms that work in your area, you can consult such a list at the office of a County Court and at a Citizens' Advice Bureau. If you feel there is a possibility that you may be eligible for subsidised legal help under the Green Form and Legal Aid schemes, it would be a good idea to consult a solicitor who undertakes this type of work from the outset. Solicitors who do operate the schemes are marked on the list of firms and you can often identify the offices of solicitors who offer this facility by a sign that they display showing two people sitting at a table with the words 'Legal Aid' written underneath.

The selection of solicitors who provide the services you require will no doubt be bewildering at first. There is no reason why you should not approach your decision in exactly the same way that you would choose a new doctor, dentist, hairdresser or milkman! If you know other people who have consulted a solicitor over similar matters, you can ask them if they can recommend him or her. Try to choose a firm that you can conveniently visit from your home or work – you may have to see your solicitor at his office on a number of occasions during the proceedings. Bear in mind the opening hours of the firm that you are considering: most firms work normal office hours so it is unusual to find a firm that is open on a Saturday. If it would be impossible for you to get to see your solicitor during working hours, you might like to investigate what his or her attitude would be to making special arrangements to see you on a Saturday or late in the afternoon. Bear in mind also that some firms close over lunchtime but others do not.

Once you have decided on a firm of solicitors, telephone them or call in and check that they can give you the sort of help you require. Ask them whether they would be prepared to take on your case and, if a particular solicitor in the firm has been recommended to you, mention that you would like him to deal with your case for you. If the firm already has all the clients it can manage, the receptionist will simply tell you, but in most cases you will be able to make an appointment to see a solicitor in the firm to discuss your case.

3. What will it all cost?

Most people are only reluctant to see a solicitor because they are worried about the cost. In fact, many solicitors will keep their charges to quite a reasonable amount in a divorce case. Furthermore, you may be eligible for help with your legal costs under the Green Form and Legal Aid schemes that exist for the benefit of those who would normally have difficulty in meeting the cost of a solicitor's advice. They are:—

a) THE GREEN FORM SCHEME

(i) *Are you eligible?*

Both petitioners and respondents are able to benefit from the Green Form scheme. Whether you are eligible for assistance will depend on your means. Both your capital and income will be taken into account. The financial limits for the scheme are altered periodically to keep pace with inflation – because of this, and because eligibility depends on each applicant's individual circumstances, it is impossible to give a definite guide as to whether you are likely to qualify or not. As a rough indication, if you are in receipt of family income supplement or supplementary benefit and you do not have very much capital, you are likely to be eligible for help under the Green Form scheme. Even if you do not qualify for either of these state benefits, you may still be entitled to assistance under the Green Form scheme provided that your income and capital are not high. The fact that you are a home owner will generally be disregarded in assessing your capital assets. Leaflets telling you about the Green Form and Legal Aid schemes and the current financial limits are printed by Her Majesty's Stationery Office and should be available free from a Citizens' Advice Bureau, the Central Office of Information, law centres, etc.

It costs nothing to ask a solicitor whether you are entitled to advice under the Green Form scheme. Just arrange an appointment to see him and tell him straight away at the interview that you are interested in the scheme. He will then take down details of your income (from earnings etc.) and your capital (for example savings, jewellery etc.) and of how many dependants you have. Using these details, he will fill in a green coloured form (from which the scheme takes its name) and he will then be able to tell you, at once, whether you are eligible for assistance. Some people will be entitled to receive their legal advice free of charge, others will be required to make a contribution towards the cost. Your solicitor will tell you whether you are required to pay anything and if so, how much. You can then decide whether you want to go ahead and take legal advice about the divorce.

Once you have paid your contribution towards the scheme, you will not be required to pay any more towards the cost of the divorce itself, not even the fee that is normally payable by a petitioner when divorce proceedings are commenced, at least until you receive your share of the family property after the divorce. However, whether you have had to pay a contribution or not, you may be asked at a later stage to reimburse the legal aid fund (which will have borne the cost of your legal advice up to that point) from any property that you receive from your spouse or manage to retain as part of your arrangements for the future. You should refer to the later section of this chapter headed 'A word of warning about the Green Form Scheme and Legal Aid' for further details of this liability (page 25).

If there are other matters to be sorted out for you in connection with the divorce (over the children, personal protection, property, maintenance etc.) you may well go on to receive help under the Legal Aid scheme. This is rather different from the Green Form scheme and you can be required to make a fresh contribution towards any legal costs that are incurred on your behalf under this scheme (see below).

(ii) *What does the Green Form scheme cover?*
The Green Form is most helpful in relation to the divorce itself. It normally entitles you to all the advice and help you will need for the divorce, whether you are a petitioner or a respondent. Most solicitors will take over the divorce proceedings for you lock, stock and barrel except that the scheme does not cover the cost of a solicitor going to court on your behalf. This means that if you are given an appointment to see the Judge to discuss the arrangements for your children after the divorce, you will have to attend it by yourself. This should not cause you any hardship as the interview will be very informal and the court will be quite used to helping people who come for the interview without their solicitor.

The scheme also entitles you to very general advice about your future arrangements. Most people require more help with these matters than the scheme provides. Further help can normally be made available under the Legal Aid scheme described below.

If you are still undecided about whether to seek a divorce and you would like to know what alternatives are available to you, this sort of advice can be given to you on the Green Form scheme – the scheme is not restricted to those who have decided definitely on a divorce.

b) LEGAL AID

(i) *Are you eligible?*
Both petitioners and respondents may be eligible for legal aid. Various financial conditions have to be satisfied, and they are very similar to those that apply with the Green Form scheme. Just as with the Green Form scheme, you are free to seek advice, without charge, from a solicitor, as to whether you qualify for Legal Aid. However, the solicitor will not be able to tell you there and then whether you qualify (although he will be able to give you a good idea) because he will have to submit your case to the Legal Aid authorities for consideration. You will normally

be required to attend an interview about your means at the offices of the Department of Health and Social Security (unless they are already satisfied with the details of your financial position because they have reviewed them in deciding whether you are entitled to family income supplement or supplementary benefit). If you are eligible for Legal Aid, your contribution towards the cost of your legal advice will be assessed. This will often be split into two parts – your maximum contribution (which is the most you could ever be required to pay) and your actual contribution (which is the amount which is expected to cover the cost of your case and is the sum you are required to pay for the moment). It is often possible to pay your contribution in monthly instalments. Once a decision has been made about your case, your solicitor will be notified and you can decide whether you want to take up the Legal Aid offer that has been made.

If you decide to take up the offer, you will not have to pay anything more immediately towards your own legal costs than your maximum contribution. However, as with the Green Form scheme, you can later be required to reimburse the legal aid fund for the cost of your legal help from any property that you recover from your spouse or manage to preserve from him or her in the course of divorce proceedings (see below).

(ii) *What is covered by legal aid?*

If you are eligible for legal aid, your solicitor will receive a certificate setting out the conditions on which it is granted to you. This will tell him exactly what work he can do for you on legal aid. You will usually find that he can do everything required to sort out all your problems associated with the divorce and this will include attending court on your behalf should this become necessary.

A WORD OF WARNING ABOUT THE GREEN FORM SCHEME AND LEGAL AID

Beware! Many people think that the Green Form scheme and Legal Aid relieve you of the responsibility for your solicitor's costs for ever. This is not always the case.

If, as part of your arrangements for the future after you are divorced, you receive some capital (be it in the form of the family home or other assets, or as a lump sum of money) you can be required to reimburse the legal aid fund from this capital for any of your legal costs that it has had to bear. You can be liable in this way even if you think that the property you get has belonged to you all along if your spouse has tried to claim a share in it at any stage in the divorce proceedings. The first £2,500 is, at the time of writing, excused from this liability nor can any claim be made on property which goes to your children or income which is paid to you as maintenance.

The operation of these provisions can be very complicated and you should ask your solicitor to explain exactly how they may affect you. Of course, the exact amount of your costs that the legal aid fund has had to bear will depend on how much your solicitor's bill for everything connected with the divorce was, how much you have paid by way of contribution to your costs, and how much, if anything, you have been able to recover towards your costs from your spouse (see below).

To give you a simple example of how the rules work, suppose that Mr. and Mrs. X decide to get divorced. Mrs. X sees a solicitor and receives advice under the Green Form scheme. She pays no contribution. The Green Form scheme pays for all her legal costs in connection with the divorce itself. She and her husband are not able to agree over their house (which is their only capital asset) or over maintenance and Mrs. X's solicitor therefore applies for Legal Aid on her behalf. This is granted and again she has no contribution to make. The Legal Aid covers the cost of all the proceedings in relation to the house and maintenance. Finally the court decides for them that Mr. X should transfer the house (which is in his name) worth £40,000 and free of mortgage, to Mrs. X and should pay her £6 per week maintenance. The total bill for Mrs. X's legal costs is £800 (an arbitrary figure which is not to be taken as a guide to the likely costs in your case). The court decides that, for a variety of reasons that need not concern us, Mr. X should not have to pay any of his wife's costs. Therefore, the legal aid fund is out of pocket to the tune of £800. Mrs. X has received property worth well over £2,500 and she will therefore be required to reimburse the legal aid fund for the whole £800. However, as the capital she gets is tied up in the house, there will be an arrangement called a 'charge' over the house. This is rather like a mortgage in favour of the fund. Mrs. X will not have to pay any interest on the amount outstanding, nor will she have to pay back any of the £800 yet. However, when she comes to sell the house, she can be required to pay back the whole £800 out of the sale proceeds unless special permission is given for the charge to be carried over onto any new house she buys.

If Mrs. X had received, say, £10,000 as a lump sum of money

instead of the house, she would have had to meet the £800 from this straight away.

Instead of being asked to reimburse the legal aid fund, you may have the pleasant surprise of receiving a refund of some of the initial contributions you have made towards the cost of your legal advice. This will normally only happen if your spouse is ordered to pay all your costs in relation to the divorce and future arrangements for you. Your solicitor will advise you what your prospects are – do not rely on getting any money back – it does not usually happen.

c) A FIXED PRICE INTERVIEW WITH A SOLICITOR

Quite a number of solicitors are prepared to give you half an hour of their time for a low fixed fee. This does not depend in any way on your income or capital. This scheme could be of advantage to you if you have one or two simple queries but it will obviously not cover the cost of legal advice in connection with the whole divorce proceedings.

A list of solicitors who will give this type of advice is available, for example, at Citizens' Advice Bureaux and at the offices of any County Court.

A Citizens' Advice Bureau may sometimes be able to arrange for you to have a short, free interview with a solicitor at their premises.

WHAT IF YOU ARE NOT ELIGIBLE FOR HELP WITH YOUR SOLICITOR'S COSTS?

What do you do if you discover that you are not able to benefit from any form of assistance with your solicitor's costs? You will then have to decide whether you wish to meet his bill from your own pocket. Do not make this decision without first investigating what he will charge you – you may be pleasantly surprised! In straightforward cases, a solicitor may be able to give you a fairly precise estimate of his charges. In a more complex matter, you can only expect a rough guide. Most solicitors are quite used to being asked about cost these days and will be as helpful as they can. You can rest assured that the days when gentlemen did not talk about money have gone for good – nowadays enquiries of this kind are considered sound good sense.

In some cases, you may be able to recover at least part of your outlay from your spouse although you should never rely on being able to do so (see below).

Substantial though your solicitor's charges may seem to be, do bear in mind that he can often save you money in the long term by making sure that your case runs smoothly and that you secure the arrangements for the future that are best for you.

RECOVERING THE COST OF YOUR LEGAL ADVICE FROM YOUR SPOUSE
CONTRIBUTING TOWARDS YOUR SPOUSE'S LEGAL COSTS

You and your spouse can, of course, come to whatever agreement you like over who is to meet your joint legal costs. However, in the absence of any agreement between you, the court can decide whether one of you should have to meet the other's expenses of any stage of the divorce proceedings. The court's decision always depends very much on the particular circumstances of your case and a book of this kind cannot therefore make any firm predictions as to the likely outcome of your case. Your solicitor may, however, be able to give you some more concrete advice on your own position.

As a general guide, a petitioner will hardly ever be ordered to pay a respondent's legal costs in relation to the divorce itself. A respondent may have to pay a petitioner's costs (although not in many cases where the petitioner has the benefit of advice under the Green Form scheme) in relation to the divorce. This will depend largely on the basis for the divorce and whether it is the husband or wife who is petitioning. Where the divorce is granted on the basis of the respondent's adultery, it is sometimes possible for the petitioner to recover some of his or her costs from the co-respondent.

If the court is called upon to decide any other matters for you, for example, custody of the children, or questions relating to property, it is quite free to make whatever order it feels is reasonable about who is to pay the costs of the particular application to the court, whether or not either of you has been receiving help under the Green Form or Legal Aid schemes. Whether you will recoup any of your costs or have to contribute towards your spouse's will depend on the attitude you have both taken to the matter in hand, who can be said to have been most successful as a result of the court's decision, how much money you each have, whether either of you have legal aid etc. etc.

4. Changing your solicitor

Most people will be quite satisfied with the service they receive from their solicitor. A few will have complaints and may want to know whether they can change to another solicitor.

You can change solicitors whenever you want to if you are meeting all your legal costs out of your own pocket. However, you will have to pay your existing solicitor's bill before he will release the papers in your case to another solicitor and without these papers, a new solicitor can really do nothing. Furthermore, it is not always wise to change your solicitor at the drop of a hat because it can cause delay whilst your new solicitor gets accustomed to your case. You should be absolutely sure that you have good reason to change.

If you are receiving the benefit of the Green Form scheme or of Legal Aid, your right to change solicitors may be rather more limited. You cannot change solicitors simply because you do not like the advice you are given, unless you have reason to believe that the advice is actually wrong. However, if you are seriously dissatisfied, you will normally be able to change to another solicitor. The best way to do this is normally to find another solicitor who you would like to consult and who is prepared to take your case on. Once you have authorised him to take over the case, he will write to the Legal Aid (or Green Form) authorities to get permission from them for the change and he will write to your former solicitor telling him what has happened and asking him to send on your papers. He will then be responsible for your case.

5. Should you consult a barrister?

A barrister is a lawyer who has been trained in a slightly different way from a solicitor. You will find that, in the legal world, a barrister is often referred to simply as 'counsel'. His job is usually associated with conducting cases in court and you will often see barristers appearing in court in their traditional wigs and gowns. Another part of a barrister's job is to advise solicitors and their clients about all sorts of legal problems.

A barrister can never be engaged directly by a member of the public. He has to be instructed to act in a case by a solicitor. It is not necessary to enlist the services of a barrister in a straightforward divorce in connection with obtaining the actual decrees of divorce. However, it is not unusual for a barrister to be instructed in connection with other problems arising in the course of the divorce, for example in relation to the children, property and maintenance. If he thinks it is necessary for you to have a barrister, your solicitor may simply go ahead and instruct a barrister for you, or he may discuss the matter with you.

If you feel personally that you would like a barrister and your solicitor shows no signs of raising the question with you, you are free to ask him about it yourself. However, many cases can be handled very adequately by a solicitor, so be prepared to accept your solicitor's advice if he says you do not need a barrister.

In suitable cases, the Legal Aid scheme will meet the cost of a barrister for you. If you are not eligible for Legal Aid, you will, of course, have to meet the barrister's fees yourself. It is wise to ask your solicitor for an estimate of what these are likely to be in advance so that you are not taken by surprise when the bill arrives.

There are a number of senior barristers called 'Queen's Counsel' who are sometimes engaged in more difficult cases. It is hardly ever necessary to instruct a Queen's Counsel (or 'Silk') in a divorce case, but if it were to become necessary, your solicitor would ensure that this was done for you. You will usually find that if a Queen's Counsel is instructed, another less senior barrister is also instructed to assist him.

If a barrister is instructed in your case, he may wish to meet you to discuss matters with you. This meeting is usually called a 'conference' and takes place at the barrister's chambers (his office) or at the court where your case is to be heard.

5
Can You Get Your Divorce Through the English Courts?

England and Wales are treated a single country for legal purposes. Scotland and Northern Ireland are separate countries and have laws that differ from those of England and Wales in many respects. 'England' is used in this chapter as a shorthand term for the whole area of England and Wales and the term 'English courts' refers to all courts throughout England and Wales.

The English divorce courts can only deal with your divorce if one or the other of you has some connection with England. You will have sufficient link with England if either:—

a) one of you is *domiciled* in England at the time when the divorce proceedings are commenced. Domicile is a legal term for a particularly close relationship between a person and a country. Your domicile is not necessarily the same as your nationality – there are complex rules for determining where you are domiciled at a given time. However, you can take it that, as a general rule, you are domiciled in the country where you have your permanent home and intend to live for an unlimited period of time. Most people who live in England are also domiciled here. But if both of you have or have had a close connection with another country (even with Scotland or Northern Ireland) which amounts to more than just taking regular holidays there, you would be well advised to consult a solicitor to check on your domiciles before embarking on divorce proceedings in the English courts, unless you are quite satisfied that one of you will be able to fulfil the conditions set out in paragraph (b) below.

or b) one of you will have been *habitually resident* in England for at least one year by the time your divorce proceedings are commenced. Leaving England for short periods, for example on a business trip or for a holiday, will not normally prevent you from being habitually resident here provided you can show that you have, at least, put down some roots here and made this your home for the year.

Provided that one of you can satisfy the domicile or habitual residence conditions, it will not matter where you got married be it in England or the other side of the world – the English courts can still grant you a divorce. An English divorce will effectively put an end to your marriage, certainly as far as your status in this country is concerned. However, if you are worried about the effect of an English divorce on your marital status in another country, it would be wise to check whether that country accepts an English divorce as valid or not. Your solicitor may be able to help, but if not, the embassy of the country in question may provide the information you require.

6
What to Expect When You Come into Contact with the Courts

There is no special family court. Most divorces are dealt with entirely by a branch of the County Court system known as the Divorce County Courts.

The Divorce County Courts

County Courts are locally based courts that can be found in many towns and cities throughout England and Wales. They do not deal with crimes but they do resolve almost every other type of problem that can arise in everyday life, for example disputes between shopkeepers and dissatisfied customers, between neighbours, between landlords and their tenants etc. etc.

Not all County Courts deal with divorce cases – those that do are known as the Divorce County Courts. It will be one of these courts that will deal with your case.

The work of deciding cases and making court orders is carried out by Judges and Registrars. Both Judges and Registrars are appointed from the ranks of senior lawyers. The chances are that most of the court orders that are made in the course of your divorce will be made by a Registrar. You may meet him personally once or twice during the case, for example if you ask the court to sort out what should happen to your property for you or to determine whether you should be paying or receiving maintenance. However, some parts of a divorce still require the attention of a Judge, for instance, the preliminary divorce decree (decree nisi) will be pronounced by a Judge and he will also be responsible for most questions that arise over your children. Most petitioners who have children will meet the Judge at least once during the divorce proceedings when they attend an informal interview with the Judge to discuss the arrangements that have been made for the children to take effect after the divorce.

There is also a large staff of court officials who are responsible for the smooth running of the court's business. Some of them are employed in the court office attached to most courts, where they deal with all the paperwork involved in County Court cases. You will meet one or two of them if you attend the court office for any reason and you will normally find them very friendly and helpful with any queries you may have. Other members of the staff are more directly involved in the day to day organisation of the court, ensuring that the court has just the right amount of business lined up to deal with each day (in so far as this is possible), checking that you, and everyone else involved in the court proceedings, are in the right place at the right time and know what you should be doing, making sure that the Judge has all the papers he needs to deal with each case etc. You may meet some of these officials, particularly the court clerk and the ushers, if you have to attend court for a hearing.

In London the equivalent of the Divorce County Court is the Divorce Registry, which is situated in the Royal Courts of Justice in the Strand.

The offices of the Divorce County Courts and the Divorce Registry are normally open on weekdays from about 10 a.m. until approximately 4 p.m. or 4.30 p.m. The courts usually hold their hearings (or 'sit') between similar hours.

The High Court

Occasionally it is necessary for a particularly difficult question that arises in a divorce case to be referred to the High Court. There are several sections of the High Court – the section responsible for divorce and other similar matters is called the Family Division.

The High Court is based in London, but this does not mean you will have to travel to London if your case is referred to the High Court. Judges of the High Court regularly visit major towns and cities throughout England and Wales to deal with cases that arise outside the London area.

The format of court hearings

Hearings connected with a divorce are dealt with either in 'open court' or in 'chambers'.

Proceedings in open court are heard in the courtroom itself. They tend to be rather formal and all the lawyers concerned will wear their legal robes for the occasion. Members of the public are normally permitted to come into court and listen to the case if they wish to do so, and the details can be reported in the press. The only matter which is likely to be dealt with in open court in the course of your divorce is the pronouncement of decree nisi of divorce – you need not usually attend for this if you would prefer not to.

Most of the divorce will be dealt with in chambers. Proceedings in chambers are heard in private, either in the courtroom itself or in the Judge's or the Registrar's own room at the court. The general public has no right to listen to any part of the case and no details can be reported in the press. Only those people who are directly concerned in the case are allowed to be present – this often means just you, your spouse, your legal advisers and the court staff. Hearings in chambers tend to be less formal and more relaxed than open court hearings and the lawyers involved will not be wearing robes.

e) that you have lived apart for a continuous period of at least five years immediately preceding the presentation of your petition ('five years separation').

These facts are explained in more detail below.

a) ADULTERY

The adultery itself

A man has committed adultery if he has had sexual intercourse with another woman (married or unmarried) whilst he is married to his wife. A married woman commits adultery if she has sexual intercourse voluntarily with a man other than her husband. Because it is essential that the sexual intercourse should be a voluntary act, a woman who is raped does not commit adultery. A sexual relationship outside the marriage that does not actually involve sexual intercourse is not adultery, although it may be unreasonable behaviour of a kind that would entitle the other spouse to petition for a divorce (see below).

You are most unlikely to catch your spouse in the act of committing adultery. Nevertheless you will be expected to prove to the court that he has done so. In many cases, he will be prepared to admit that he has committed adultery and this makes your task quite straightforward. The court can be informed of the respondent's admission very simply. When he first receives the divorce papers from the court, he will also be sent a form of questionnaire called an acknowledgement of service. One of the questions on the form asks him if he admits that he has committed adultery. If he answers this question affirmatively, the court may be prepared to accept this as sufficient proof.

If the respondent is not prepared to admit adultery, your task may be considerably harder. You will have to produce evidence to the court proving that he has committed adultery. In this situation it is quite common for an enquiry agent (private detective) to be engaged to keep watch on the respondent. The enquiry agent can then inform the court of any circumstances that strongly suggest that adultery has taken place, for example he may be able to give evidence that the respondent spent the night alone with another woman at her house, or that the respondent and another woman booked into a hotel as 'Mr. and Mrs. Such and Such', taking only one double bedded room. Sometimes it is not necessary to instruct an enquiry agent at all because you are already in possession of evidence that strongly points to adultery. For example, you may have found correspondence between your husband or wife and another woman or man in terms that make it clear they have been having a sexual relationship, or you may have discovered that your husband or wife is in possession of contraceptives that you know he or she never uses when you have sexual intercourse together. In the case of a wife, it may be possible to prove that she has become pregnant at a time when you could not have had sexual intercourse with her, perhaps because you were away on a prolonged business trip, or ill in hospital. Obviously, the evidence available will be different in each case – these are just examples to give you an idea of the type of evidence that the courts normally expect.

People are often worried about disclosing the name of the other man or woman involved in the adultery. This may be because they do not appreciate that nowadays divorces attract virtually no publicity – the days when big divorce suits attracted large crowds to the court and made the headlines in all the papers have gone for good. The reason for this is that, as you will see from Chapter 9, most divorces are now granted by a special procedure which means that the names of those involved are unlikely to be mentioned more than once or twice in court in public, and no details of the case are given at all. In the majority of cases, therefore, it would be foolish to be worried about informing the court of the name of the other person involved. If you do know the name, you must tell the court in your petition. If, on the other hand, you do not know the name of the other person, the respondent is not prepared to disclose it to you, and you cannot reasonably be expected to find it out, a divorce can be obtained on the basis of adultery with a 'person unknown'.

If you mention the name of the other person involved in the adultery in your petition, that person is entitled to take part in the divorce proceedings in so far as they affect them. The proper term for such a person would then be the 'co-respondent'. The court will provide the co-respondent with copies of all the relevant divorce papers and he or she will have the opportunity to confirm or deny anything said about him or her in the divorce proceedings.

Providing that it is intolerable for you to live with the respondent
Proving the adultery is only the first step. You have to go on to satisfy the court that you find it intolerable to live with the respondent any more. Strange though it may seem, it is not essential that you find it intolerable to live with the respondent

because of his adultery. Of course, in many cases the two things are bound up together. On the other hand, it may be that your marriage has been unhappy for some time before the adultery takes place and everything has combined to make it intolerable for you to go on living with the respondent.

Living together after you find out about the adultery

If, after you find out about the respondent's adultery, you live together as man and wife for a period exceeding six months, or for several periods which together add up to more than six months, you will not be able to rely on that adultery to obtain a divorce. This is not to say that you cannot make attempts at a reconciliation: as long as the period (or periods) during which you live together do not exceed six months in total, the court will completely disregard them in considering whether you should be granted a divorce. Furthermore, a new six month period will be allowed after each fresh act of adultery is discovered. So, suppose that at the beginning of 1985, you discover that your husband has been committing adultery with Samantha Bloggs but you nevertheless go on living with him as his wife for the whole of 1985 – you would not be able to rely on this adultery in seeking a divorce. However, if you were to discover in, say, January 1986 that your husband committed adultery again in December 1985 with Samantha Bloggs or with any other woman, you would be allowed a further six months living with your husband before you would lose your right to claim a divorce based on the December 1985 adultery.

b) UNREASONABLE BEHAVIOUR

The behaviour

Although people have generally come to talk about getting a divorce because of their spouse's 'unreasonable behaviour' (and the term is also used in this book), this is not strictly an accurate description of the type of conduct that must be proved before a divorce can be obtained. The law actually says that you must show that your spouse has behaved in such a way that you cannot reasonably be expected to live with him or her. The court will make an individual judgment in your case as to whether you should have to go on putting up with your spouse's behaviour. The final decision will depend on what sort of people you both are and on all the circumstances of your case. It is not possible to lay down hard and fast rules about the type of behaviour that will and will not justify a divorce, nor can you conclude that just because a friend or relative was granted a divorce on the basis of a particular kind of conduct by his or her spouse, you would necessarily obtain a divorce because your spouse has behaved similarly. However, as a guide to the sort of standard that the court will apply, it is certainly not sufficient that you simply do not get on with your husband or wife any more or that you have come to the conclusion that you are totally incompatible and should never have got married. Every marriage suffers from its minor irritations and it is rare to find anyone who does not have one or two complaints to make about their spouse. It is only when the behaviour of your spouse goes beyond the ordinary wear and tear of married life and begins to cause serious problems in the home that the court will step in to grant a divorce.

There are a number of types of behaviour that frequently crop up in some shape or form as unreasonable behaviour. They range from violence and threats of violence to persistent abuse, nagging, drunkenness, neglect, refusing to have sexual relations, indulging in sexual perversions, associations with other men or women outside the marriage, placing unreasonable restrictions on the personal freedom of the other spouse, failing to provide the other spouse with sufficient money etc., etc. In some cases, even relatively trivial incidents can be too much to expect a husband or wife to put up with if they happen repeatedly during the marriage.

How do you judge whether you can be expected to go on living with your spouse? It is easy to lose all sense of proportion when your marriage is breaking down and to take it for granted that the reason for all your problems is that your spouse is behaving in an unreasonable manner. However, it is not sufficient that you personally think so – you have got to satisfy the court as well. It may help you to look at your situation rationally if you ask yourself these two simple questions:—

'Would an outsider who did not know me or my spouse think that my spouse was behaving towards me in such an unreasonable manner that I should not be expected to have to go on living with him/her?' If your answer to this first question is 'Yes', then the conduct of which you complain may well be serious enough for you to obtain a divorce. If your truthful answer is 'No', you should ask yourself a second question:

'Is there anything out of the ordinary about me or my spouse or our particular circumstances that makes my spouse's behaviour unreasonable though it would not be in most cases?' If you can answer this question affirmatively, then you may still be entitled to a divorce because the court will be prepared to take into account the personalities of yourself and your spouse. To take an extreme example, suppose that you are a very confident person and very keen on insisting on your rights. You may think it perfectly right that your husband complains in a loud voice in public places whenever the smallest detail does not meet with his complete satisfaction. Indeed you may find it excessively irritating if your husband was not prepared to speak up in this way. But, if you are a very shy and retiring person, you may find this type of behaviour quite unbearable and extremely upsetting and the court would bear this in mind. If, on top of your own character, you could show that your husband behaved in this way largely in order to upset you, you may find that the court would be ready to accept that you should not have to go on living with him and to grant you a divorce. Of course, things can also work the other way and the circumstances of the particular marriage can turn conduct that would otherwise be unreasonable into conduct that is understandable and acceptable. To take another example, let us suppose that both husband and wife are Catholics. The wife, being very anxious not to become pregnant again, insists on using contraceptives when they have sexual intercourse. The husband, on religious grounds, feels that this is wrong and refuses to have sexual intercourse with her at all in these circumstances. In some cases, an outright refusal to have sexual intercourse could be regarded as unreasonable behaviour. But in the light of the husband's religious beliefs, the court may well accept that he is not in fact being unreasonable. Furthermore, the court can also take account of the way in which *you* have behaved. So if, for example, you have behaved just as badly as your spouse or have provoked him or her into unpleasant conduct towards you, the court may feel you have simply got exactly what you asked for, and may refuse to grant you a divorce.

The fact that the respondent's behaviour is caused by an illness from which he is suffering will not necessarily prevent it from being unreasonable, although the court would normally expect that, up to a point, you should accept and share the burdens imposed on the family by the physical or mental ill health of one spouse.

For one spouse simply to leave the other would not normally

amount to unreasonable behaviour. (Although in such a case it may be appropriate to seek a divorce on the basis of a period of separation or desertion – see the following paragraphs.) However, if the departure is accompanied by other unpleasant conduct, the court may be prepared to decide that you cannot be expected to live with the respondent in the future and to grant you a divorce.

Does it matter that we are still living together?

As with adultery, your right to claim that you cannot be expected to go on living with your spouse will not be affected by the fact that you have, in fact, lived with him whilst the behaviour of which you complain was taking place or even after it occurred, *provided* that the period (or periods) during which you live together do not total more than six months. If you live together as man and wife for a period (or periods) in excess of six months after the last incident of which you complain, the court will take this into account in deciding whether you can be expected to go on living with the respondent in the future as well. It will not necessarily mean that you will not get your divorce but you will normally be expected to show that there was some good reason why you continued to live with the respondent – for example, you may have had to do so because you were unable to find alternative accommodation.

c) DESERTION

Proving that your spouse has deserted you for a continuous period of at least two years immediately before you petition for divorce can be a very complicated matter. The following paragraphs will give you a broad outline of what is involved; if you are seeking a divorce on the basis of desertion, your solicitor will check that you can comply with the rather complex legal requirements upon which the court will insist before granting you a decree.

Fortunately it is not often necessary to rely on the fact that your spouse has deserted you when you seek a divorce. This is because desertion very often happens as a result of other problems that have arisen in a marriage and there is therefore usually another basis on which a divorce can be granted. For example, if your spouse has deserted you and you have been separated for at least two years, there is a good chance that he too will have decided that he would like a divorce – if so, you will be able to obtain your divorce on the basis of your two years separation and his consent to the decree. Or your spouse may have deserted you after behaving unreasonably for some time, in which case you will be able to obtain your divorce by satisfying the court that he has behaved in such a way that you cannot be expected to go on living with him any more. If you find yourself able to prove this, you will not even have to wait for two years separation to elapse before pressing on with divorce proceedings. Another quite common reason for one spouse to leave the other is that he or she has found someone else and wishes to set up home with them. Here again, you, as the deserted partner, will not have to wait for two years to pass before taking divorce proceedings as you may well be able to prove that your spouse has committed adultery and obtain a divorce on this basis straight away.

What is desertion?

The simplest form of desertion is where one spouse simply walks out on the other spouse one day for no reason at all. However, desertion is not just a physical separation of husband and wife. It implies that the deserting spouse has completely rejected all the normal obligations of marriage. This means that the court will have to be satisfied of the following things:—

(i) two years living separately - you must show that you and your spouse have been living separately for a continuous period of two years immediately before you started the divorce proceedings. Usually the separation comes about when one of you leaves home, but the situation can arise where you are living separately even though you are both still living under the same roof. This will be the case if one of you cuts yourself off completely from the other so that you are no longer living as a married couple. The court is very strict in deciding whether you have reached this state of affairs and will need to be satisfied that you no longer do any of the things together or for each other that married couples normally do, such as eating together, spending your leisure time together, carrying on a sexual relationship, sleeping in the same bed, cooking and washing and doing odd jobs for one another etc. (This principle is also adopted under (d) below in determining separation for the following ground, two years separation and consent.)

Although the law requires that you should have been separated for a continuous period of two years, it would be wrong to discourage you from trying to patch things up in the meantime if you wish to do so. Therefore, the court generally disregards short periods during the separation, during which you have lived as man and wife again in an attempt at reconciliation. However, you will not be able to count such periods as part of the two years separation that you will have to show before you can get your divorce. So, for example, suppose that a year after you first separated, you spend a month living together again in an attempt to make a success of your marriage again. It is no better than before however and you part again. The month you have spent together will not normally prevent you from starting to count your two years separation from the time your spouse first deserted you. On the other hand, you cannot count it as *part* of the required two years and you will therefore have to wait until two years and one month have passed from the date of the first desertion before you can seek your divorce. If, on the other hand, you live together for a period or periods totalling more than six months at any stage after your first separation, the court will be able to take this into account in deciding whether you can establish the relevant period of desertion and the chances are that you will not therefore be able to obtain your divorce on this basis or at least not without encountering further delay.

(ii) that your spouse has decided that the marriage is over you must also show that when he stopped living with you, your spouse viewed the marriage as ended and intended to remain separated from you permanently. This will often be clear from the way he behaved or from things he said at the time. It means that there will be no desertion where, for example, your spouse only intends a temporary separation or where he still looks upon himself as a married man but has to go away for some reason, for instance because of his job.

You will *not* be able to complain that your spouse has deserted you if:–

(i) you consented to the separation the mere fact that you breathe a sigh of relief as soon as the door closes behind your husband or wife does not mean that you have given your consent to the separation. But in some cases, you may be taken to have consented even though you never actually discussed the matter with your spouse or gave your consent in so many words. This could happen if you have made it clear from your comments or your behaviour that you are agreeable to the separation. This means, for example, that if you ask your husband to leave and he does so or if you decide between you that you should live apart, you will not be able to turn round later and complain that he has deserted you.

(ii) your spouse had good reason to leave – there may be a perfectly acceptable or neccesary reason for your spouse leaving, for instance he or she may have to go into hospital for long term treatment or may even be committed to prison for a criminal offence. This would not be desertion unless your spouse also looked upon the marriage as finished and never intended to come back to you even when he or she was able to do so. Furthermore, your spouse may be quite justified in leaving because of your own behaviour, for example if you commit adultery. If you are to blame in this way, you will not be able to complain of desertion. You will get a picture of the type of behaviour that might put you in the wrong if you read the preceding section dealing with unreasonable behaviour – any behaviour on your part that could be classed as unreasonable behaviour is likely to excuse your spouse from any blame if he walks out on you.

How does desertion end?

In some cases, your spouse's desertion will come to an end and you will no longer be able to rely on it in claiming a divorce. This will happen, in many instances, if you get back together again on a permanent basis or if your spouse makes a genuine offer to return to you permanently which it would be reasonable for you to accept and you refuse to do so. Because desertion is a state of affairs that only exists when the separation is against your will, it is also true that if you change your mind and come round to the idea of living apart, and you and your spouse actually come to an agreement that this is what you will do in the future (possibly by drawing up a separation agreement), you will no longer be able to complain that he has deserted you.

d) TWO YEARS SEPARATION AND CONSENT

If you wish to rely on this basis for your divorce, you will have to prove that you and your spouse have been living apart for a continuous period of two years, just as you must show this if you wish to claim a divorce on the basis that your spouse has deserted you.

The separation

The circumstances in which the law looks upon you as having

been separated for the requisite period can include not only periods when you are living in separate places but also times when you are living in the same house but in two separate households, and are more fully described on page 43 under the heading *'What is desertion?... (i) two years living separately'*. Short periods during which you live together will not affect the continuity of your separation provided that they do not exceed six months in total. However, just as with desertion, you will not be able to count these periods towards the two years separation required. If you live together for a period or periods totalling more than six months, you will not be able to rely on any period of separation that preceded your cohabitation as justifying a divorce, and, if you separate again, you will then have to wait for a further two years to elapse before you can seek a divorce unless you have other grounds for claiming a divorce (adultery or unreasonable behaviour).

At first glance, you may wonder whether there is any difference between two years separation and consent, and desertion. The most obvious difference is, of course, that you will not be granted a divorce on the basis of two years separation that does not amount to desertion unless your spouse is prepared to give his consent to the divorce; whereas, if you can show that he deserted you, you can obtain your divorce whether he agrees to it or not. Why should there be this extra requirement of consent? The reason is that desertion is based on the idea that your spouse has been at fault in separating from you and that you are therefore entitled to a divorce irrespective of his feelings about the matter. On the other hand, if you can satisfy the court that you both want the divorce, all it will need to know is that you, or one of you, made a decision at some stage that the marriage was over and you were going to part for good, and that since then you have lived separately for at least two years – no question of blame comes into it and you will get your divorce even if you were both fully in agreement about the separation. The type of separation that will never be enough for a divorce is the sort of situation where you both intend to start living together again as soon as you can do so in the future – this will rule out, for example, most separations that come about for reasons simply of business, ill health and even imprisonment.

The consent

There are strict rules about proving that your spouse consents to the divorce. It is not enough that, when you ask the court for the divorce, he raises no objections – he must actually signify his consent to the court. His consent will only be valid if he gives it quite freely without any pressure being brought to bear on him and with full understanding of what the divorce will mean to him. He will normally find it convenient to tell the court of his consent when he completes the questionnaire known as the acknowledgement of service which the court will send him as soon as you have started divorce proceedings. The court always sends a set of notes with the acknowledgement of service form, which explain clearly the consequences of giving consent to the divorce and what the granting of a divorce means. The form is simple to fill in and all your spouse is required to do to give consent is to answer affirmatively the question asking whether he consents to a divorce being granted, sign the form and return it to the court.

If your spouse will not consent to the divorce and you cannot prove that he or she has deserted you (or committed adultery or behaved unreasonably), you will have no choice but to wait until five years separation has elapsed before you seek a divorce, (see below).

If you are the respondent in a divorce of this type, you should be quite sure that you do understand what a divorce will mean to you personally before you give your consent. Even after you have signified your consent to the court, you are free to withdraw it again without any explanation at any stage before the preliminary divorce decree, decree nisi, is pronounced but it is vital to inform the court (and preferably your spouse as well) if you intend to do this. Between decree nisi and decree absolute of divorce you will only be able to withdraw your consent in quite exceptional circumstances. After decree absolute has been obtained, the divorce is final and you will no longer be able to withdraw your consent.

Special protection for respondents

In relation to divorces granted on the basis of two years separation and consent and five years separation (see below), the courts have special powers to protect the financial and personal position of the respondent and they can sometimes delay or even prevent the granting of a divorce to make sure that he or she will not suffer because of it. You should refer to Chapter 11 for an outline of the court's powers in this respect.

Generally

A divorce based on two years separation and consent should present very few problems to either spouse. Many people do seek their divorces on this basis and it is the nearest we have come, in this country, to divorce by mutual consent. It has the great advantage that neither of you has to show that the other has been to blame in any way for the breakdown of the marriage.

e) FIVE YEARS SEPARATION

If the separation between you has gone on for five years or more, the court will grant you a divorce whether or not your spouse is prepared to agree to it. Apart from the longer period of the separation and the fact that consent is not required, the case will be exactly like that described above based on two years separation. The court will look upon you as living separately in exactly the same circumstances and you will be able to live together for short periods (not totalling more than six months) without breaking the continuity of the five year period in just the same way. Should you live together for more than six months, the five year period will only start to clock up once you separate again – you will not be allowed to rely on any time that preceded your cohabitation. You should refer to Chapter 11 for details of the court's powers to protect the personal and financial position of respondents in this type of case.

8 Starting the Divorce Proceedings

1. YOUR FIRST VISIT TO THE SOLICITOR

If you intend to take legal advice about your divorce, there is no point in delaying your first visit to a solicitor. As soon as you make up your mind to seek a divorce (or even before, if you would like some advice about your decision), make an appointment to see the solicitor you have settled on.

Each solicitor develops his own methods and style over the years so everyone will find their first interview slightly different. It may simply be a preliminary chat that gives you a chance to meet the solicitor and gives him the opportunity to find out roughly what you will need help and advice on. If so, you will probably be asked to make another appointment for some time in the near future so that you can discuss your situation with your solicitor in more detail. On the other hand, some solicitors prefer to get down to business straight away and may spend an hour or so with you, taking down information about your case and giving you a run down of what to expect in the divorce proceedings. It is always a good idea to leave yourself plenty of time for this first visit so that you can relax and take in everything your solicitor says and ask him about anything that is troubling you.

There are certain things that almost every solicitor will do at your first or second appointment:–

Dealing with the cost of your legal advice

a) If he thinks you may be eligible for help under the Green Form scheme (see Chapter 4), one of the first things he will do is to assess whether you qualify. He will need to ask you about your finances in order to do this, so you can help him if you look out details of your income (from employment etc.) and your capital (savings in cash or the bank etc., premium bonds, stocks or shares, jewellery, furs etc.) before your first appointment so that you are able to answer his questions accurately and precisely. If you are eligible for help with your legal costs under this scheme, he will tell you straight away. He will also tell you whether you are required to contribute anything towards the costs yourself, and if so, how much. If you then decide that you would like him to advise you, and you are prepared to pay the contribution, you will be asked to sign the application form he has filled in for you. You may be required to pay the full amount of your contribution there and then.

b) If you do not qualify for assistance under the Green Form scheme, you will be able to ask about the cost of legal advice so that you can decide whether you wish to pay for legal help yourself. If you decide to do so, you can tell your solicitor that you would like him to act for you and you can sort out how much money he will require you to pay in advance.

c) If your solicitor thinks you may be eligible for help with your legal costs under the Legal Aid scheme (see Chapter 4), he will have to fill in an application form for you at some stage. He may well decide to do so soon after you first consult him to avoid delays later on. This will enable him to get the application off for processing in good time, and you will hear in several weeks time whether you have been granted legal aid or not and how much you will be required to contribute yourself.

Finding out about you and your marriage

a) Your solicitor may ask you if there is any possibility of you and your spouse getting back together again. If you feel this is out of the question, you are quite free to say so. However, if you are still undecided about things, tell your solicitor. He may be able to raise the question of reconciliation with your spouse for you, or suggest where you might seek help in making a fresh start with your marriage.

b) You will be asked to give various details of your marriage, for example, where and when it took place, how many children you have and when they were born, when and where you last lived with your husband or wife, whether there have ever been any other court proceedings in relation to your marriage or your children (for example, you may have made an application in the magistrates' court for maintenance in the past, or perhaps one of your children was adopted by you). If you have a copy of your marriage certificate, it can be helpful if you take it to your solicitor, but if you do not have one, don't worry – your solicitor will help you to get hold of one.

c) Your solicitor will need to know what complaints you are making about your marriage and why you want a divorce, for example because your spouse has committed adultery and you cannot bear to go on living with him or her or because your spouse has behaved so unreasonably that you cannot go on living with him or her.

d) You may well be asked about your own and your spouse's financial position – how much capital do you both have, what do you each earn, is your spouse giving you anything towards your own and the children's expenses or are you giving him or her any money, can you manage on what you have, etc? Do not worry if you do not know any details of your spouse's financial position – your solicitor will be able to find out in due course, if it becomes necessary to do so. Your solicitor is also likely to ask you about the matrimonial home and whether you have come to any agreement about who should live there at present and what should happen to it once the divorce comes through. There are a lot of things a solicitor can do to help with accommodation and money in the early stages of a divorce (for example by explaining what state benefits might be available to you, or by making an application to the court for an order that your spouse should pay you a regular sum of maintenance until the divorce takes effect). If you feel you need help with anything, therefore, raise it with him as soon as possible, even if he does not raise the point himself. Tell him also if you are in difficulties over the children or if your spouse is harassing you in any way; he may be able to resolve problems of this kind for you too. (You can get a picture of the sort of thing that can be done from the later chapters of this book.)

e) You will be expected to provide an address at which your spouse can be contacted so that he can be notified of the divorce proceedings and sent all the relevant divorce papers. You may not know where your spouse is living – this is not usually a major obstacle as your solicitor will be able to take steps to trace him or, if this proves impossible, he can often make arrangements for the divorce to go ahead nevertheless.

Putting you in the picture

a) Once he has all the information that he needs from you, your solicitor will be able to advise you whether you have grounds for a divorce. If you do, he will tell you something about the procedure involved in obtaining a divorce and he may be able to give you an idea of how long it is likely to take before decree nisi of divorce comes through. If there are any details you particularly want to know, do not be afraid to ask.

b) If your solicitor discovers that you do not yet have grounds for a divorce, he will be able to advise you what alternatives are available to help with your particular problems.

c) You may well be advised that it is best, once you have finally decided on a divorce, if you try to live completely separate from your spouse (for example you should no longer be sleeping with him, cooking for him, eating with him, etc.). This is just to make sure that you do not prejudice your chances of getting a divorce.

2. THE PREPARATION OF THE DIVORCE PETITION AND THE STATEMENT AS TO THE ARRANGEMENTS FOR THE CHILDREN

a) The divorce petition

Once your solicitor has all the details he requires, he will be able to get on with the next step – preparing the divorce petition. A divorce petition is required in every case. It is the formal legal document that will form the basis of your claim for a divorce. Your solicitor will set down in it details of your marriage and your children and the grounds on which you are seeking a divorce and he will list the claims that you will be asking the court to consider (for example, you may want the court to deal with financial matters for you or to grant you custody of the children). Your present address will be included in the petition as a matter of course. (If you are seriously anxious that you will be in danger if your spouse finds out in this way where you are living, mention this to your solicitor so that he can advise you whether a special application to the court for permission to leave your address out of the petition would be in order in your case.)

When your solicitor has drafted the petition, he will ask you to read through it to check that all the information he has included is correct. It is most important that you are very careful about this because it can cause serious problems and delay if information later turns out to be inaccurate and the petition needs correcting. It is easy to exaggerate incidents that have occurred during your marriage – you should be sure that you have not given your solicitor the wrong impression about events that he has described in the petition because you will be required to prove that everything in your petition is true. If you have any doubts or queries about anything, raise the matter with your solicitor before you agree to the petition.

b) The Statement of Arrangements

If there is a child or children of your family, another document, known as the 'statement as to arrangements for children' (or simply the 'statement of arrangements'), will also have to be prepared at this stage. This sets out the arrangements you propose for the children once the divorce is granted.

A 'child of the family' is any child who is a child of both of you, or who has been adopted legally by both of you, or any other child who has been treated by both of you as part of the family (except a child boarded out with you by a local authority or voluntary organisation). Generally the court is not concerned in divorce proceedings with adult children who can take care of themselves, and you will not have to give any details of the arrangements (if any) for them. But you will be required to provide details of the arrangements for any children who are under 16, or who are under 18 and are still receiving instruction at an educational establishment or undergoing training for a trade, profession or vocation (whether or not they are in paid employment as well). Exceptionally, the court requests details of the arrangements for older children, for example if they are seriously physically or mentally handicapped.

You will need to have information available for your solicitor about any arrangements you have made so far as to where the children are to live, who else will be living there with them, who will look after them, where they are to be educated or what employment they have, what financial arrangements are proposed for them, what arrangements have been made for the other parent to see them (or for you to see them, if they are to live with your spouse), whether they have any illnesses or disability and whether they are under the care or supervision of any person or organisation such as a welfare officer.

When your solicitor has filled in the statement of arrangements from these details, he will ask you to check it through for errors. Be very thorough about this – the Judge will generally have to be satisfied that your proposed arrangements are suitable before you can obtain your final decree of divorce, decree absolute, and he will base his consideration of the matter substantially on what you say in the statement of arrangements.

3. FILING THE NECESSARY PAPERS IN THE COURT OFFICE

Divorce proceedings are actually started by filing (or formally presenting) the appropriate documents at the office of a divorce court. The court office will require:—

a) the completed divorce petition (and a copy for your spouse);

b) the completed statement of arrangements, if you have any children of your family of the relevant ages (and a copy for your spouse);

c) a copy of your marriage certificate – your solicitor will tell you how best to obtain one if you have not got a copy;

d) in some cases, a fee for starting the proceedings. This is payable unless you are receiving help with your legal costs under the Green Form scheme or drawing supplementary benefit or family income supplement. If you fall into these categories, you can apply to be excused the fee.

Your solicitor may ask you to file these documents at the court yourself or he may send or take them to the court for you.

Once the court receives the documents, it will give your case a reference number. The divorce proceedings are now under way.

9
Obtaining Decree Nisi

The court now takes charge of proceedings for a while. In most cases, the court will address all communications about your case to your solicitor and he will inform you about the progress that is being made.

1. Serving the papers on the respondent (and co-respondent)
Once the petition and accompanying documents have been filed with the court, the court office sends a copy of the petition and the statement of arrangements (if appropriate) to the respondent. This process is described as 'serving' the documents on the respondent. He will also receive two further forms from the court with the divorce papers – the 'acknowledgement of service' and the 'notice of proceedings'.

a) THE NOTICE OF PROCEEDINGS
This informs the respondent that divorce proceedings have been commenced against him and explains that he must return the completed acknowledgement of service form within eight days. He is warned that if he intends to instruct a solicitor, he should take all the divorce papers to the solicitor of his choice who will complete and return the acknowledgement of service for him. It also gives him instructions to assist him in filling in the acknowledgement of service himself if he does not wish to consult a solicitor.

b) THE ACKNOWLEDGEMENT OF SERVICE
This is a document in question and answer form which is primarily designed to enable the court to be certain that the respondent has been served with the divorce papers and is fully aware of the divorce proceedings. The court will not proceed with your case until it is sure that, if it is possible to notify the respondent, he does know that proceedings have been

commenced and has details of the proceedings. The respondent is required to confirm on the form that he has received the divorce petition. He is also required to answer questions about his attitude to the divorce, in particular whether he intends to defend the case, and what his reaction is to the claims you have made in your petition (for example for custody of the children).

If you have based your divorce petition on your spouse's adultery and have named the other person involved, that person is the co-respondent in the divorce suit and is entitled to be notified of the divorce proceedings. He or she will also receive a notice of proceedings and an acknowledgement of service and must return the completed acknowledgement of service to the court.

2. Where the respondent (and co-respondent) return the acknowledgement of service to the court indicating that they do not wish to defend the divorce – and the special procedure.
Very frequently, the respondent (and co-respondent if there is one) return the acknowledgement of service as instructed indicating that they do not intend to defend the divorce. The procedure that follows is quite straightforward:

a) The court will send your solicitor a copy of the completed acknowledgement of service together with copies of two more printed forms known as the 'request for directions for trial (special procedure)' and the 'affidavit of evidence (special procedure)'. The term 'special procedure' refers to the relatively new, streamlined method of obtaining a divorce. Until fairly recently, all petitioners seeking a divorce had to appear in open court and give evidence before a Judge about their marriage and the reasons why they were claiming a divorce. This is no longer necessary in most cases because the court hearing has been replaced by written evidence confirming the details contained in the divorce petition. Some people, usually those with no children, can now obtain a divorce without ever having to visit the court at all.

The affidavit of evidence – this is the document used to confirm that all the details given in your petition are true, or in other words, the document that proves your case to the court. The affidavit is in questionnaire form and is designed to contain one or two more details about the matters you mentioned in your petition. Your solicitor will fill it in for you. He will ask you to have a look at the signature on the respondent's acknowledgement of service and confirm that this really is your spouse's signature – you will be required to state that this is so in the affidavit. Your solicitor may feel that it would be wise to support what you have said about your marital problems in your petition and affidavit with evidence from another person and he may want to discuss this with you. For example, he may want to know whether your doctor would be able to give the court a report on injuries that the respondent inflicted on you. Any evidence that your solicitor decides should be submitted to the court on your behalf will be put in a written form and will be sent to the court with your affidavit.

Your solicitor will give you the completed affidavit to read through – you must be very sure that the contents are accurate because you will then be asked to take an oath that everything in the affidavit is true. This procedure is called 'swearing' the affidavit. It is done either at the offices of another solicitor (on payment of a small fee) or at the court office (where no fee is payable). The fact that the affidavit has been sworn will be recorded at the end of it and it will be signed by the solicitor or court official in front of whom you took the oath. Whatever you say in your affidavit is just as much your evidence to the court as if you had stood in the witness box in the court room and stated the facts to a Judge out loud.

The request for directions for trial – your solicitor will complete this very simple form requesting the court to proceed with your case.

The request for directions for trial and the affidavit of evidence are returned to the court by your solicitor. It is then up to the court to set in motion the next stage of the proceedings.

b) Once the request for directions for trial and the affidavit of evidence have been filed with the court, the next step is for the Registrar to consider your case and decide whether he is satisfied that you have proved that you should be granted a divorce. You do not normally have to attend when the Registrar considers your case but you will be notified, via your solicitor, of his decision. *If the Registrar is happy with the case*, he will give his certificate that you are entitled to a decree of divorce. If you have asked for the costs of the divorce to be paid by the respondent or co-respondent (see Chapter 4) the Registrar will also consider this claim and anything that the respondent or co-respondent has had to say about it in the acknowledgement of service. If he is satisfied that you are entitled to the costs you claim, he will state this in his certificate. If he is not satisfied about your claim to costs, he can refer the matter to the Judge who will be pronouncing your decree nisi of divorce. The party who is objecting to your claim to costs will then be notified that he should ttend at court on the day fixed for the pronouncement of the decree nisi to put his point of view to the Judge. He may also be ordered to provide a written statement of his objections.

c) When the Registrar has given his certificate that you are entitled to a divorce, a date will be fixed for decree nisi to be pronounced in open court by the Judge. Although you and the respondent (and co-respondent) will be told when this is to take place, you do not need to attend unless there is any dispute over costs which has to be dealt with by the Judge. If there is such a dispute both you and the party who is raising the objections to your claim should attend to explain the matter to the Judge. This should rarely be necessary but if it is, your solicitor will give you instructions as to what you should do and say.

d) You are free to go along to court to hear your decree nisi pronounced if you wish. If you decide to do so, you may be rather disappointed by the lack of ceremony involved – the whole procedure is likely to be over in a matter of minutes. The Judge or a clerk of the court reads out a list of the names of the couples who are to be divorced that day – you will hear your own name mentioned in this list. The Judge then announces that decree nisi of divorce is granted in each of the cases named. As soon as he has done this, you have completed the preliminary stage of the divorce by obtaining decree nisi.

e) Whether or not you decide to attend court for the pronouncement of decree nisi, you and the respondent (and co-respondent) will be sent a copy of the decree by the court. Your copy will probably reach you via your solicitor. You are *not* yet divorced – the decree nisi is simply a provisional decree of divorce and has to be converted into the final decree of divorce, or made 'absolute', at a later stage. It is only when decree absolute has been granted that your marriage is at an end and you are free to remarry (see Chapters 12 & 25).

f) *If the Registrar is not satisfied that you are entitled to a divorce* when he considers your case, he can either give you the opportunity to produce further evidence in support of your case, or he can refer the whole case to the Judge for him to decide whether you should be granted a divorce. If the matter is referred to the Judge, the special procedure will no longer be applicable and you will have to attend at court on a day which will be fixed for consideration of your case to give evidence personally to the Judge of all the details contained in your petition. The Judge will then decide whether to grant your divorce. This procedure is not often needed these days. If your case has to be dealt with in this way, you can apply for Legal Aid to cover the cost of legal representation by your solicitor or a barrister at the hearing, provided, of course, you fall within the limits of the Legal Aid scheme. If you are not eligible for Legal Aid, you will have to pay your solicitor to represent you but there may be some prospect of recovering your outlay, or some of it, from the respondent or co-respondent – your solicitor will advise you about this. There is no need to worry about the hearing itself. It is normally quite brief and very straightforward, and your solicitor will tell you exactly what to do. You should not jump to the conclusion that, just because your case cannot be dealt with by the special procedure, this means that you will not get your divorce. Of course, divorces are sometimes refused, but it is more likely that the Judge will be able to grant you a decree even though the Registrar refused to give his certificate.

g) If, for any reason, you are refused a divorce, you should take your solicitor's advice as to whether there is any prospect of successfully renewing your application at a later date and as to the courses of action that are available meanwhile to help you resolve your difficulties despite the court's refusal to grant you a divorce (for example, you may wish to apply for a maintenance order, or for a sale of the family home to be ordered because you are in need of capital, or for custody of the children to be sorted out).

3. Where the respondent (or co-respondent) returns the acknowledgement of service to the court indicating that he intends to defend the case.

If the respondent (or co-respondent) indicates in the acknowledgement of service that he wishes to defend the proceedings, your next step will depend on whether he files with the court a formal document called an 'answer' setting out his objections to your petition. He normally has 29 days after first receiving your divorce petition and the accompanying documents in which to file his answer with the court, although it is sometimes possible for a respondent or co-respondent who decides at a later stage that he wants to defend the case to file an answer even after this period has elapsed.

a) WHERE AN ANSWER IS FILED

If an answer is filed, the court will notify your solicitor and send him a copy of it. The special procedure can no longer be used. Unless the respondent (or co-respondent) changes his mind about defending the case, there will eventually be a hearing in open court at which you and the respondent (and the co-respondent) will be expected to attend and give oral evidence to a Judge, who will consider whether, in the light of what you all have to say about the matter, a divorce should be granted. It is very rare for a divorce to reach this stage nowadays, however determined your spouse (or the co-respondent) may be to prevent the divorce being granted. No further details are therefore given in this book of the rather complicated procedures that are involved in a defended divorce. You, as the petitioner, would almost certainly be granted Legal Aid to help with your legal costs of the defended divorce (provided your means are within the limits of the scheme). You would therefore be able to rely entirely on your solicitor to guide you through the proceedings. Unfortunately, you will usually find that, if the case is defended, quite considerable delays can be experienced in obtaining your divorce.

If you are a respondent (or co-respondent) and you are contemplating defending the proceedings, perhaps because you do not agree that your marriage has broken down irretrievably, or because you disagree with some of the things the petitioner has said in her petition, you are strongly advised to consult a solicitor before committing yourself in any way. Defending divorce proceedings can be a fruitless exercise that simply wastes the time and money of all concerned, without conferring any advantage on you. A solicitor will explain whether you have any prospect of defending the case successfully and what steps you can take, short of defending the divorce, if you disagree with any of the matters raised in the petition. If you do not wish to be divorced because you feel there is still a chance that you and your spouse could make a success of the marriage, you can talk over the question of a reconciliation with the solicitor, and he can raise the possibility of attempting a reconciliation with your spouse on your behalf.

If your solicitor feels that it would be worth your while to defend the petition, he will advise you how to go about this and whether you will be eligible for Legal Aid to cover the legal costs involved (which can be substantial). However, it is only right to point out that it is very hard to obtain Legal Aid to defend a divorce these days, however small your means.

b) WHERE NO ANSWER IS FILED

Not infrequently, the respondent (or co-respondent) indicates in the acknowledgement of service that he wishes to defend the case but then fails to file an answer within the 29 days allowed after he received the divorce papers. If this happens, the case will be dealt with by means of the special procedure as if the respondent (or co-respondent) had never intended to defend it. Your solicitor will be able to check with the court, once the requisite period has elapsed, that it is in order to proceed in this way. He will then obtain from the court the two forms mentioned above, the affidavit of evidence and the request for directions for trial. The procedure thereafter is exactly the same as that described above in relation to a case where the respondent (or co-respondent) indicates in the acknowledgement of service that he does not want to defend.

4. Where the respondent (or co-respondent) fails to return the acknowledgement of service.

If the respondent (or co-respondent) does not return the acknowledgement of service as required, proceedings will usually be delayed whilst arrangements are made for someone (often a court official called a court bailiff, or some other independent person such as an enquiry agent) to visit the respondent (or co-respondent) and make sure that he receives copies of all the relevant papers. This procedure is known as 'effecting personal service' of the documents.

Once it is possible to satisfy the court that the respondent (and co-respondent) have notice of the case, the normal procedure can be put into operation to obtain the divorce decree.

Sometimes it is impossible to trace the respondent to serve him with the divorce papers, for example because you do not know where he is living. Although difficulties of this kind can give rise to delay, they are not normally insuperable. If necessary, the court can be asked to make an order permitting you to proceed with your petition even though you have been unable to trace your spouse to inform him of the divorce proceedings.

10
After Decree Nisi: The Judge Considers the Arrangements for the Children

The procedure described in this chapter will apply to families with children. If you have children, the following paragraph will tell you whether it applies to you.

1. The court's duty in relation to children
The court has a duty to make sure that suitable arrangements are made for certain categories of children when their parents get divorced. If you have children of the family (see Chapter 8) who are under 16 or are under 18 and in education or training, you will not normally be able to finalise your divorce by converting your decree nisi into decree absolute until the court has considered the arrangements you propose for these children and declared that is is satisfied with them.

Some families include older children who are still dependent on their parents because they have special problems, such as mental or physical handicaps. If the Judge feels that it is necessary to do so, he can assume responsibility for older children such as these, as well as for any younger children you may have, and check up on the arrangements you have made for them. The court will give a special direction if the Judge intends to do this.

2. The respondent's views about the arrangements
You, as the petitioner, provide the court with details of the arrangements that you propose for the children when you complete and file with the court the statement of arrangements at the commencement of the divorce proceedings. The respondent receives a copy of this with your divorce petition. He is then free to make his own views about the proposed arrangements known to the court if he wishes.

A respondent who wishes to do this should write promptly to the court setting out the matters he wants to raise. This letter should reach the court, if possible, within eight days after he receives the divorce papers. It must obviously reach the court before the Judge considers the arrangements for the children. The respondent will be informed when the Judge will be considering the arrangements and can attend, if he wishes, to put his own views to the Judge in person.

It is particularly helpful for the respondent to inform the court of all that he knows about the arrangements for the children if you and he have agreed between you that he is to look after the children on a permanent basis in the future, rather than you.

If the respondent does write to the court commenting on the arrangements for the children, your solicitor will receive a copy of his letter from the court, so that you are aware of his views.

3. Special procedure cases: the children's appointment with the Judge.

a) WHEN IS THE APPOINTMENT LIKELY TO TAKE PLACE?

The arrangements for the children are always considered by a Judge. Unless you are in dispute with the respondent over custody or access or any of the other arrangements for the children, an appointment for you to see the Judge will be fixed automatically by the court, and you will be informed, through your solicitor, when and where to attend. The respondent will also be informed so that he can attend if he wishes. The appointment is often fixed for the same day as the pronouncement of your decree nisi. If this is arranged in your case, you may like to consider attending a little earlier for your appointment so that you can hear the decree being pronounced. However, this arrangement is not always possible, and there may be some days or weeks delay after your decree nisi is pronounced before the Judge can consider the arrangements for the children.

It is essential for you to attend the appointment with the Judge unless you have an exceptional reason for not doing so. You will be given details of whom to contact in case of difficulty when you receive notice of your appointment. If you cannot attend on the day fixed, it is most important that you or your solicitor contact the appropriate person (usually at the court office) so that they can try to rearrange your appointment. If you simply fail to turn up on the day, there will be a delay whilst another appointment is arranged for you and this may prevent you from making your divorce final as soon as possible.

If you and the respondent are in dispute over any of the arrangements for the children, you are unlikely to be notified of an appointment to see the Judge. Instead, your solicitor will be informed that he may apply specially for an appointment to be fixed for you. He will be able to judge whether it is worth applying for an appointment before you have resolved your difficulties with the respondent. If there is a serious dispute between you, the Judge may not be able to declare himself satisfied with your arrangements until it is sorted out and it would therefore be a waste of his time and yours to discuss the arrangements until then. On the other hand there may be cases where the Judge would be prepared to declare himself satisfied even though you are still in dispute, for example if you are fighting over the custody of the children but you would both provide first class homes for them and you are sensibly not letting your disagreement affect the children in any way. Furthermore, if it appears that there is likely to be considerable delay before all the problems over the children are resolved, the Judge may be prepared to give limited approval to your arrangements to enable you to finalise your divorce. The practice of individual Judges may well vary substantially where there is an outstanding dispute between you and the respondent. (If the respondent is looking after the children, he may have to attend the interview with the Judge as well as or instead of you. Exactly what is arranged will depend on the practice of your local court. In any event, you will always be able to attend and make your views known to the Judge just as the respondent can when you are looking after the children.)

b) WILL MY SOLICITOR ACCOMPANY ME?

Only if you pay for him yourself, since the Green Form scheme does not cover this, although you may be eligible for Legal Aid (if you qualify) if there are serious problems over the children.

Generally, you should have no difficulty in coping with the appointment on your own. The whole procedure is very informal and is geared for people who do not have a solicitor with them. Your solicitor will advise you what to do before you go along for the appointment and, if you are particularly worried, he can smooth the path for you by, for example, writing to the court before your visit, explaining any special problems there may be about your case. Some solicitors even accompany nervous clients to the appointment out of the goodness of their hearts!

c) GOING TO COURT FOR THE APPOINTMENT

When you attend for your appointment, you should take with

you a copy of your statement of arrangements (which you can obtain from your solicitor). You may find it useful to take a copy of your petition with you as well. If you have received a copy of any comments that the respondent has made to the court on the proposed arrangements, you should also have this with you. The Judge will have his own copies of all these documents and he may wish to refer to them.

When you arrive at the court building, you should ask to be directed to the place where the children's appointments are being heard. Your appointment will take place in the Judge's private room at the court, which is normally situated close to the court room itself. Once you have found the right place, you may well find that there is a list posted, showing all the cases that are to be dealt with that day, and you should check that your own name is mentioned. It is always a good idea to let a court official know that you have arrived; there is usually someone at hand, dealing with everyone who is attending court that day. You can ask the official where you should wait for your appointment. If you wish to hear your decree nisi being pronounced, and you have been notified that this will be done on the same day as your appointment, you should ask the official where to go to hear this. Make sure that you arrive early for your appointment and leave yourself plenty of time free to remain at court for several hours if necessary. Even though you may have been given a specific time for your appointment, the court can never promise that it will take place exactly on time. This is because urgent matters sometimes crop up that require the Judge's immediate attention and more routine matters have to wait their turn, whereas, at other times, cases take much less time than anticipated and your appointment can be dealt with earlier than arranged.

d) WHAT WILL HAPPEN AT THE HEARING?

When the Judge is ready to consider your case, you will be called into his room. The hearing is private and the only people present will be you (and the respondent if he attends), the Judge, and one or two court officials. It is not likely to take very long. The Judge will probably ask you some questions about the proposals for the children that you have outlined in your statement of arrangements, and about the welfare of the children generally, and you should be prepared to volunteer information yourself about any changes that have been made in the arrangements since the statement of arrangements was prepared.

When the Judge has covered all the matters about which he needs to know, he will tell you whether he is prepared to approve your arrangements.

e) THE ORDERS THE JUDGE CAN MAKE

Unqualified approval: in most cases, the Judge will simply say that he accepts that your arrangements are satisfactory or that they are the best that can be devised in the circumstances. Your solicitor will receive a copy of the official order to this effect through the post so that you can go ahead and apply for your decree nisi to be made absolute when the time comes.

Where unqualified approval cannot be given: sometimes the Judge is not prepared to give his unqualified approval to your arrangements. There are various reasons why he may come to this decision, for example he may feel that he does not know enough about your proposals or he may not be prepared to approve them because you and the respondent are in disagreement over custody or access or other arrangements, or he may take the view that what you propose will be unsuitable for the children, or that specific problems, for instance over accommodation, should be ironed out before he gives his seal of approval. There are a number of alternative courses of action he can take in these circumstances, for example:

i) he can ask you to return for another appointment and provide him with further information generally or about specific aspects of your arrangements. Sometimes the date of the new appointment will be fixed there and then, sometimes it will be left up to you to apply for an appointment when you feel that you are in a position to provide the Judge with the information he requires.

ii) he can refer the case to the court welfare officer for investigation and a report, if he feels that the problem is something you cannot resolve for him yourself. The court welfare officer is an independent person, experienced in dealing with this kind of job. He will probably want to visit your home and possibly that of the respondent, and he may want to see the children. He will also need to talk to both of you. When he has collected all the information he needs, he will prepare a written report for the Judge. You will be notified when the report is ready and you are entitled to see a copy of it, as is the respondent. You or your solicitor can obtain a copy of it from the court office. A fresh appointment is not normally arranged until you apply to the court office for one. The Judge will then reconsider his decision in the light of the welfare officer's report.

iii) he can put off his final decision until a particular problem has been resolved. For example, you may be waiting for a long promised council house so that you do not have to live in overcrowded conditions with the children, or you may be just about to complete the purchase of a new property so that you can provide a proper home. In this sort of case, you may be given the date of the new appointment straight away, or it may be left up to you to apply for a fresh appointment when the particular difficulty has been sorted out.

iv) he may decide to give limited approval in one of the forms described below, so that you can go ahead and obtain your decree absolute.

If the Judge refuses to give approval to your arrangements, consult your solicitor straight away. He will advise you whether you can get Legal Aid to cover the cost of him sorting things out for you. Even if you are not entitled to Legal Aid, he will be able to give you further advice and help under the Green Form scheme if you have been receiving assistance under the scheme or are eligible to do so.

Limited approval: even if the Judge is not prepared to give unqualified approval to your arrangements, there are two alternative orders that he can make that will still entitle you to obtain your decree absolute. He can order:

i) that it is impracticable for you and the respondent to make any arrangements yourselves for the children. This may be appropriate where, for example, your children are not living with you or the respondent, perhaps because they are in the care of the local authority.

or ii) that you should be permitted to go ahead and finalise your divorce without delay, even though he cannot approve the arrangements you have made for the children. The Judge will only make this order if there are exceptional circumstances making it desirable that you should be granted decree absolute; permission to proceed in this way is rarely given. Furthermore, it can only be given if the court is confident that the whole question will be brought before the Judge again at a later date so that he can reconsider your arrangements. You or the respondent or both of you will therefore be required to give an undertaking to the court that you will raise the question of the arrangements with the Judge again within a specified time so that he can check that he is satisfied with your revised proposals.

4. Cases not dealt with by way of the special procedure. The preceding section applies only to those divorces which are dealt with by means of the special procedure (i.e. without a hearing of the divorce case in open court – see Chapter 9).

By far the majority of cases are now dealt with by special procedure, but there are still a few that are referred for a full hearing in front of the Judge for one reason or another. If this happens, the question of the arrangements for the children will often be considered in open court at the same time as the divorce itself, rather than at a separate appointment. The orders that the Judge can make are just the same as those described in this chapter, section 3 (e) above. If your case has to be heard in this way, your solicitor will represent you at the hearing and will give you all the detailed advice you need about it.

11
Special Protection for the Respondent Against the Divorce or its Consequences

In every divorce case, whatever the ground on which the petitioner seeks the divorce (adultery, separation etc.), the respondent has the right to defend the case and oppose the granting of the divorce if he or she feels that the petitioner cannot justify his or her claim, for example because the marriage has not broken down irretrievably or because the petitioner is unable to prove the facts set out in his or her divorce petition. You can find details of this right to defend in Chapter 9.

However, if you are claiming a divorce on the basis either (i) that you have been separated from the respondent for two years and he or she consents to a divorce; or (ii) that you have been separated from each other for five years, the respondent is given additional protection against the divorce being granted without full consideration being given to the financial and other consequences that it may have for him or her.

In the majority of cases, it is the wife who seeks to prevent or to hold up the divorce on the basis of the consequences that it would have upon her. Therefore (contrary to the practice adopted in the rest of this book) this chapter is written on the assumption that the husband is seeking a divorce and the wife is the respondent seeking protection against it. Exactly the same principles apply, however, where the husband is the respondent.

1. How the wife can occasionally prevent a divorce where the divorce petition is based on the fact of five years separation. If you petition for divorce on the basis that you have been living separately from the respondent for five years (see Chapter 7), and you cannot prove any other fact that would entitle you to a divorce (such as adultery or unreasonable behaviour on her part), the respondent has a special right to oppose the divorce on the basis that, if it were granted, she would suffer *grave financial or other hardship* and that it would be *wrong in all the circumstances to permit the divorce*. If the court supports her argument, it can refuse to grant you a divorce.

Grave financial or other hardship: the breakdown of a marriage inevitably causes some hardship to both spouses. This hardship alone will not give the respondent sufficient grounds to prevent the divorce. The court will only refuse a divorce on the basis of hardship if it is shown that the hardship will arise from the actual divorce itself, rather than simply from your separation or the breakdown of your marriage. Furthermore, it will be necessary for the respondent to prove that the hardship she will suffer will be very serious indeed. Therefore it will normally be very difficult for her to prevent you from obtaining a divorce on the basis of hardship.

Financial hardship can take a variety of forms. It includes not only present hardship, but also the loss of the chance to acquire a future benefit that the respondent might acquire if the divorce does not take place. For example, a woman might argue that she would suffer financial hardship if the divorce went through because she would lose her rights to a very favourable widow's pension at some stage in the future were you to die first.

Before the court concludes that the respondent will suffer financial hardship, it has to look at all the circumstances. It may be, for instance, that the loss of one benefit will be compensated by the acquisition of another that the respondent will get after the divorce but would not have been entitled to had the marriage continued. For example, a wife losing the prospect of a state widow's pension through divorce may be entitled to receive supplementary benefit making her income up to roughly the same amount instead.

Even if the court does feel that the respondent will suffer grave financial hardship if the divorce is granted, it will not refuse the divorce outright. You will be given the opportunity to put forward proposals to compensate her. For example you might offer to purchase an annuity for her to replace a pension she would have received from your employers had your marriage continued until your death.

Other hardship is particularly difficult to establish. It is sometimes argued that a respondent will suffer grave other hardship where, in her own community, she would become a social outcast after the divorce because of the prevailing social and religious attitudes to divorce. However, it is not enough for the respondent to argue that the divorce will cause her personal unhappiness, or that she considers it to be morally wrong.

Wrong in all the circumstances to grant the divorce: if the respondent satisfies the court that she will suffer grave hardship (whether financial or other) as a result of the divorce, the court will still only refuse to grant your divorce if it is satisfied that it would be wrong in all the circumstances to dissolve your marriage. In coming to its decision, the court will bear in mind all sorts of factors, for example, how you have both behaved, the interests of any children involved, the reasons why you particularly want to be divorced etc.

It is rare for a divorce to be refused on the basis of hardship as described in this section. However, even if she fails to *prevent* a divorce being granted on the basis of harship, the respondent still has the right to *hold up* the final decree of divorce until you can satisfy the court that you have made proper financial provision for her for the future. The procedure whereby she can seek to do this is described in the following section.

2. Holding up the divorce where the petition is based on two years separation and the respondent's consent or on five years separation.

If you seek your divorce on the basis of two years separation and consent, or on the basis of five years separation, and you are unable to prove any other fact that would entitle you to a divorce, the respondent will be able to hold up the making of the final decree of divorce (decree absolute) until the court has reviewed her financial position as it will be after the divorce and satisfied itself that you have done all you should to provide for her.

The respondent has to make a special application with the help of her solicitor to have her financial position considered in this way before the divorce is finalised. If she does make an application, this will not prevent you from obtaining decree nisi of divorce, but you will not normally be able to finalise the divorce by obtaining decree absolute until later on unless the court can be satisfied either (i) that you should not be required to make any financial provision at all for the respondent or (ii) that the financial provision you have made for her is reasonable and fair, or the best that can be made in the circumstances.

In deciding whether it is sufficiently satisfied, the court will consider all the circumstances of your case, including your ages, health, conduct, earning capacity, financial resources and financial obligations. It will also have a look at how the respondent is likely to stand financially if you should die first after you are divorced.

Sometimes the respondent's right to hold up the divorce can work unfairly against a petitioner who has a good reason for wanting to finalise the divorce (for example so that he can re-marry) and who has every intention of making proper provision for the respondent, but for some reason is unable to do so straight away. The court does have the power, therefore, in special circumstances, to permit the divorce to be made absolute even though it is not yet satisfied with the financial provision that has been made for the respondent. It will only do so if it feels that it is desirable that you should be divorced without delay, and you will be required to outline the arrangements that you are proposing for the respondent's financial support to the court for its approval and to undertake that you will make the provision that you propose.

As you will see in later chapters, the court has very extensive powers to make orders *after* the divorce to ensure that justice is done between you in relation to property and maintenance (for example, it can order that one of you maintain the other, or that you sell the house and divide the proceeds between you). Most couples do call on the court to make orders of this kind at some stage during their divorce. However, enlisting the court's help in this way is not the same as the application described in this section for special *prior* consideration of the respondent's financial position after divorce.

An application of the type described in this section can be

made only by a respondent in a divorce based on a two or five years separation, and, if it is made, this will hold up the final decree of divorce until the court has investigated the whole matter.

In the more usual type of application described in later chapters, any petitioner or respondent can seek assistance from the court and the making of the application has no effect whatsoever on the timing of the divorce itself decree absolute can be obtained in the normal way even if there are still problems over property and maintenance to be resolved.

In many cases the respondent will be just as anxious as the petitioner to be divorced and will therefore prefer to let the court sort out problems over finances etc., in the normal way, without holding up the divorce itself. For some, however, the right to prevent the petitioner from finalising the divorce until he has made suitable financial provision can prove a valuable way of putting pressure on him to do something about the financial side of the divorce at an early stage.

It is important to have advice from a solicitor on the rather special applications described in this chapter, whether you are a petitioner or a respondent. If you think application under either heading might affect your case, you can seek general legal advice about it under the Green Form scheme (provided you fall within the financial limits of the scheme). If you are a petitioner faced with an application by your spouse for special consideration of the effects of the divorce on her, you may well also be entitled to Legal Aid to meet some or all of the costs of full legal representation by your solicitor on this point (provided that you qualify financially for help under the scheme). In just the same way, a respondent who is advised to make such an application may also be eligible for Legal Aid for full representation.

12
Obtaining Decree Absolute

Decree nisi is only a provisional decree of divorce. Your divorce becomes final when decree nisi is confirmed (made absolute) by the court.

When can decree nisi be made absolute?

There are several conditions that must be fulfilled before decree nisi can be made absolute:

a) Decree nisi cannot normally be made absolute until at least *six weeks* after the date on which the decree nisi was granted.

In very exceptional cases, it is possible for decree nisi to be made absolute before the six week period has elapsed. This is called 'expediting' the decree absolute and special permission is required from the court before it can be done. Permission is very rarely granted but if you feel there are good reasons why the court should permit you to finalise your divorce within a shorter period than normal, you should raise the matter with your solicitor as soon as possible (preferably even before your divorce petition is filed) so that he can advise you on your prospects of obtaining special permission and can make the necessary application to the court if he thinks it is worthwhile.

b) If you have children of the family whose welfare has to be considered by the court, you will not normally be allowed to apply for the decree to be made absolute until the arrangements for them have been considered by the Judge and he has declared himself satisfied with them or has ruled that it is impracticable for you to make any arrangements for them. However if there is a particular reason why you should be allowed to finalise your divorce without further delay, the Judge can give you special permission to apply for your decree to be made absolute despite the fact that he is not yet satisfied with the arrangements you have made. You will find further details of the provisions relating to arrangements for your children in Chapter 10.

c) If you have obtained decree nisi of divorce on the basis of two years separation and consent or five years separation, the respondent can make a special application to the court to have his or her financial position after divorce considered. If the respondent makes such an application in your case, you will not be allowed to have your decree made absolute until it has been dealt with. This type of application was described more fully in Chapter 11 – do not confuse it with the far more common application made by most spouses, requesting the court to sort out their finances and property after divorce for them. The fact that you or your spouse have asked the court to make financial and property adjustment orders of this latter kind for you will not prevent you from obtaining decree absolute, even if the questions you have raised have not yet been resolved.

How to apply

The application to have decree nisi made absolute is very straightforward. Your solicitor will assist you with it, or may even make the application on your behalf. It involves completing a simple form (obtainable from the court office) which is then returned to the court office dealing with your divorce. Once your form has been handed in, the Registrar will check that all the conditions described above are fulfilled. If everything is in order, the Registrar will grant decree absolute. You or your solicitor and the respondent will then be sent a copy of the official order. Keep it safely – it shows that your marriage has been finally dissolved. You may need to produce it to prove that you are divorced, for example if you wish to get married again in the future.

Do not leave it too long before applying for decree absolute

If you allow more than twelve months to pass between obtaining decree nisi and applying for decree absolute, your application must be accompanied by a written explanation for the delay and you may be required to explain the delay in an affidavit to the Registrar. If you cannot satisfy him that you have a reasonable explanation, he can refer the matter to a Judge and you will be required to explain to his satisfaction before you are granted decree absolute.

Can a respondent apply for decree absolute?

If the petitioner does not apply for decree nisi to be made absolute within three months of the time when she could first have applied, the respondent is entitled to take the matter into his own hands and apply for decree absolute himself. The procedure is slightly less straightforward than when the application is made by the petitioner, because a short court hearing in front of the Registrar will be required instead of a simple application form.

PART 3: PERSONAL COMFORT AND SAFETY AND OCCUPATION OF THE HOME

13
Personal Protection and Occupation of the House

If you are lucky, you and your spouse may be able to go your separate ways as soon as you realise that your marriage is at an end. Or you may, at least, manage to tolerate each other until the divorce is over and arrangements can be made to share out your property so that you can each find yourself somewhere to live.

But you may be less fortunate. You are both likely to be tense and emotional, perhaps even bitter, because your marriage is breaking down. You may start to get on each other's nerves and you may well have no choice but to live in the same house because neither of you is able (or willing) to find somewhere else to live. In this sort of situation, relations between you can become increasingly strained. You may never have thought that you or your spouse were capable of unpleasant behaviour or violence towards each other but you may find that you begin to torment and try to hurt each other, perhaps by taunting, or abuse, or threats, or even with physical violence – anything from the occasional push or slap to more serious assaults.

Do you stay and put up with it? Or do you move out and tackle the apparently insuperable problem of finding temporary accommodation? You already know the problems you are up against if you stay at home; if you move out there will be other snags to contend with – who, for example, will take you in? What will happen to the children if you take them with you? What will happen to them if you don't? How will you get to work and the children to school?

Some people are not even fortunate enough to have any choice in the matter – their spouse simply turns them out of the house against their will.

The courts are able to help considerably with all these sorts of problems, and this chapter outlines the type of thing the court can do to tide you over until matters improve.

What can the court do to help?

Alice's case is a good example of the help that the court can give.

Alice and Bill were married in 1970. They have three children. They were fairly happy when they were first married but then things started to go wrong after their third child was born. Bill began to go out every night, leaving Alice to look after the children. He did not come in until late, and when he did return, he was often drunk. As relations between Alice and Bill got worse, he started to drink more and could not get up in the mornings. In the end he lost his job for bad time keeping and could not find another. From then on he began to spend his time at the pub and the betting shop and he never had any money to give Alice for housekeeping. He began to take things out on Alice; at first he just shouted at her and abused her, but some time ago he came in drunk one night and hit her about her face and body. From then on he was violent to her quite frequently. Once he pushed her over so that she hit her head against the cooker and had to have stitches for a cut on her forehead.

Alice was at the end of her tether and was frightened for herself and the children. She decided that she would have to move out of the house – Bill threatened that he would throw her out anyway if she did not go of her own accord. She took the children and went to her mother's. Her mother has not got a very big house and conditions with three children all under 10 years old were overcrowded so they could not all go on living there very long. Her mother also lives in a different area which made it awkward for Alice to get to work and it took half an hour to get the children to school each morning.

Bill telephoned repeatedly, mostly in the middle of the night, to ask Alice to return. When she refused to do so, he threatened her and her mother. Alice saw him hanging around at the end of her mother's road on numerous occasions. She did not feel that she could go back to live in the same house as Bill with things as they were. Nor did she feel that she could cope with the situation as it was. She decided she would have to seek assistance from the court.

Alice needed two kinds of help. She needed somewhere suitable where she and the children could live, and she needed to be protected from Bill. The court was able to give her both sorts of assistance.

As Alice was looking after the children, it was obviously most practical if she lived in the family home with them. The only question was whether she could go back to live there with Bill if the court stepped in to prevent him from harming her and generally making a nuisance of himself, or whether Bill would have to leave so that Alice and the children could live in peace. The court made an order preventing Bill from distressing Alice by using violence or threats or other unpleasant conduct towards her. It considered making a similar order preventing Bill from harming or tormenting the children, but decided that there was no real danger that he would do so anyway. The court then considered the question of the house. It also decided that it was necessary to exclude Bill from the house completely so that Alice could go back to live there. Because Bill had hung around Alice's mother's house, the court additionally took the view that there was a danger that he would be inclined to come back to the matrimonial home and hang around upsetting and annoying Alice. It therefore made an order prohibiting him from coming within a specified distance of the house.

If Alice and Bill had had a fairly large house, there may have been a half way measure open to the court – it could have regulated what part of the house Bill should be allowed to use, leaving the rest of the house for Alice and the children. For example, if there had been five bedrooms and two bathrooms, the court could have ordered Bill to keep to one of the bedrooms and one bathroom. Together with an order prohibiting Bill from interfering with Alice in any way, this might have been enough to tide the family over until the divorce came through and their property could be sorted out so that they could each make arrangements for a home of their own. As it was, Bill moved out of the house within the time limit set by the court and went to live with his mother. Although he found it hard, he obeyed the court order and kept out of Alice's way completely so that he could not be tempted to annoy her or hurt her in any way. However, he was able to arrange to see the children every week.

How do I go about getting help from the court?

Help is available from either the Magistrates' Court or the County Court. Husbands and wives are equally entitled to be protected by the court, although it is more common for a wife to seek help. This chapter therefore assumes that it is the wife who is applying to the court; the same principles apply where a husband seeks help. In some cases, it may be appropriate for each of you to ask the court to intervene in some way. For example, you may each require protection against the conduct of the other. If the circumstances warrant it, there is no reason why the court should not deal with applications from both of you at the same time.

It is not necessary for either of you to have started divorce proceedings before you apply. Nor is it essential that you are still living together – some of the most acute problems are likely to arise when one of you has been expelled from the home by the other. Furthermore, it does not matter who owns the house, or in whose name a tenancy is.

If you genuinely feel you need help, the first step is to consult your solicitor *without delay*. It will be far more difficult to convince the court that you really do need protection if you have left it for some time after the last incident before you try to do something about the situation. The exact nature of the assistance the solicitor will be able to obtain for you depends on the court to which your application is made. Your solicitor will decide which is the appropriate court.

Help from the Magistrates' Court

a) The Magistrates' Court can make orders protecting you or a child of the family from your spouse. These are called 'personal protection orders'.

Before you can get a personal protection order, you will have to satisfy the court:

(i) that your husband has used violence or threatened to use violence against you or a child of the family and

(ii) that you need to be protected from him by an order of the court.

If you can satisfy these conditions, the court can make an order preventing your spouse from using or threatening violence against you and/or a child of the family.

b) The Magistrates' Court can also make an order excluding your spouse from your home. This is called an 'exclusion order'. However, the magistrates will only make an exclusion order if your case is serious.

If your husband has already been violent towards you or a child of the family, you must be able to show that you or the child are in danger of being physically injured by him, or would be if he were to be allowed into the home.

If your husband has not actually been violent towards you or a child yet, you will have to show:

(i) that you or a child are in danger of being physically injured by him and

(ii) that he has threatened you or a child with violence and by doing so he was breaking an existing personal protection order already in force, or alternatively, that he has threatened you or a child with violence and he has already demonstrated that he is capable of violent behaviour by using violence on someone else.

If necessary, when it makes the exclusion order the court can also order your husband to allow you to return to live in the home. This might be appropriate, for example, if there was a serious risk that your husband would move out as directed but at the same time change all the locks so that you could not get back into the property.

Help from the County Court

There is a wider range of orders available from the County Court. They fall into two categories – 'non-molestation' orders and 'exclusion' orders. The technical name for an order of either type is an 'injunction'. Magistrates' orders are not referred to as injunctions.

a) *Non-molestation injunctions*: – the court can make an order prohibiting your spouse from 'molesting' you or the children. This is roughly the equivalent of the Magistrates' Court personal protection order, although the County Court is able to protect you not only from violence but from a wider range of behaviour on the part of your spouse.

Many people think that 'molestation' means simply violence. In fact the term covers a multitude of sins (the dictionary defines molesting someone as 'meddling' with them). The court can step in to prevent all sorts of anti-social behaviour by your husband towards you or the children. Alice's case provides an illustration of the type of conduct that can often justify a non-molestation injunction – actual violence, threats of violence, frequent and distressing abuse, disturbing the whole family by coming in late at night in a drunken and noisy state, repeatedly telephoning at unsocial hours, hanging around in an attempt to argue with and abuse the other spouse etc. – in fact any conduct whereby your spouse makes a serious nuisance of himself towards you or the children. However, you should be careful not to cry wolf! You will be expected to put up with a fair amount of unpleasantness and irritation as a result of the breakdown of your marriage before the court will step in.

b) *Exclusion injunctions*: – the court can exclude your spouse from the family home and even from the immediate vicinity of the house and can also order him to permit you to return to live there if he has turned you out, or is preventing you from entering.

The court will not make this type of order unless it considers that it is fair, just and reasonable in the circumstances of your case. There are all sorts of factors to be taken into consideration including the behaviour of each of you, and both your personal circumstances – for instance, what, if any, alternative accommodation you would each be able to find if you had to leave, whether either of you will suffer injury to your physical or mental health if you have to go on living in the same house etc. If you have children, the court will concentrate particularly on how the situation is affecting them. It will want to know how much it is distressing the children to see the relationship between you and your husband deteriorate; what effect it would have on them if your husband was ordered to leave and how they would be affected if he was to stay; whether they are, in fact, being directly involved in the breakdown of your marriage, perhaps because your spouse has threatened violence towards them or because you cannot help drawing them into arguments between you. The court will also need to know which of you is to look after the children if it orders that one of you should move out of the house – if you cannot make this decision yourselves, it may have to make a decision for you.

When the court has all the information it needs, it is likely to approach its decision on the house in two halves. It will first decide whether the situation has got so bad that you can no longer go on living together as a family in the same house. If it considers that this point has been reached, it has then got to decide how things can be arranged so that you and your spouse do not come into contact any more than is necessary. If you have only got a small house, there may be no choice but to order one of you to move out. If you have more room, it may be possible for the court to divide up the house and allocate part to each of you so that you do not get under each other's feet. Either way, the court will have to decide who is to move out or who needs most space in the house. If you have children, the court's decision will usually be determined by what is going to happen to the children. The parent who is going to look after them will normally be allowed to stay in the house whilst the other spouse will have to move out. If there are no children, the court will decide what should be done by looking at the way you have both behaved and assessing which of you would be better able to fend for yourself if turned out of the home. If one of you has obviously behaved far more unreasonably than the other, that spouse can usually expect to be the one who is ordered to leave. Rest assured, however, that there is no danger of the court ordering *you* to leave when you have applied for an exclusion injunction against your husband, unless he actually asks the court to exclude you. Most husbands do not attempt to have their wife excluded, but argue simply that they should not have to leave the house as you can still manage to live together.

If there is a serious possibility of your husband making a nuisance of himself in the vicinity of the house at any time after he has been ordered to leave, the court can be asked to make a further order prohibiting him from coming within a specified distance of the house, for example, he may be ordered not to come within 50 yards of the house, or to enter the road in which it is situated.

As with a non-molestation injunction, it is worth remembering that an exclusion injunction will not be granted just for the asking. Indeed it is even harder to satisfy the court that it should grant an exclusion injunction – when all is said and done, you are asking the court to exclude a man from his home, and you will have to satisfy the court that the situation in your home goes well beyond the normal disturbance and irritation that can be expected as part of a marriage breaking down before it will do this.

Will I have to attend court to get the order?
Yes, you will have to attend court to give evidence about your circumstances and you may also have to swear an affidavit setting out in writing the reasons why you need the court's help. Your husband will normally also have an opportunity to give evidence at the court hearing, and if there is time before the hearing, may file an affidavit setting out his side of the story.

How long will the court's order last?
It is up to the court to decide how long its order should last. It will generally specify the duration of the order when it makes it.

Personal protection orders and non-molestation injunctions if you need personal protection when you or your husband have already started divorce proceedings, your application will be to the Divorce County Court for a non-molestation injunction. You can generally expect this to last until you are divorced although the court can grant an injunction for a shorter or longer period.

If you have not embarked on a divorce and do not anticipate doing so in the near future, you can apply either to the County Court or to the Magistrates' Court. You will find that the Magistrates' Court actually fixes a time limit for its order. The County Court may also do so, but may leave the duration of the injunction rather more open by simply specifying that it should last until the court makes a further order in the case. It will not make a further order unless you or your husband specifically ask at a later date that the injunction should be altered or discharged.

Exclusion orders and injunctions: on the whole, these are likely to cause greater inconvenience and therefore do not last for as long as personal protection orders and non-molestation injunctions. They are not intended to resolve the question of your accommodation for good but to tide you over until you can make alternative arrangements or take divorce proceedings so that the court has an opportunity to deal with long term arrangements for your family property. A maximum of three months is generally considered to be sufficient time for the order to last. If you are still in difficulties at the end of the injunction, it is usually possible to apply to the court to extend the period of its order.

If either of you want the terms of the order or injunction (of whichever type) varied or the injunction discharged completely, for instance because you have become reconciled since it was made, you are free to ask the court to make a further order.

Living together whilst the court's order is in force

Non-molestation injunctions and personal protection orders do not necessarily mean that you will be living separately; they simply regulate your conduct towards each other. On the other hand, an exclusion order or injunction will, of course, mean that you will be living apart. However, if you both want to give things another try and start living together again, you are perfectly free to do so without referring back to the court. If your husband feels that in these circumstances he would prefer not to have the exclusion order hanging over him, he can apply to the court to have it discharged because it is no longer appropriate.

Seeing the children when the court order is in force

Provided your husband has not specifically been prevented by the court from seeing the children he will normally be entitled to do so even though a personal protection order or non-molestation order is in force or he has been excluded from the home. However, you may have to be prepared to alter your arrangements over access to make sure that they do not involve your husband in breaking the court's order. For example, if your husband has been ordered not to come within 50 yards of the house, he will not be able to pick the children up at the door and you may have to arrange for a neighbour or relative to take them to the end of the road to meet him.

How quickly can I get an order?

In a normal case, the court will not deal with your application until your spouse has been notified of it and given a chance to attend at court to put his side of the story. However, if you urgently need help because you or a child of the family are in imminent danger of being seriously injured by your spouse, the court can act immediately without your spouse even knowing that you have made an application. If the court makes an emergency order in this way, the order is described in the County Court as an 'ex parte' order; in the Magistrates' Court, the order is called an 'expedited order'. As a general rule, you will not be able to obtain an exclusion order by this emergency procedure the only protection you will be given will be in the form of a non-molestation injunction or personal protection order. In a really urgent case, it is possible to apply to a Judge of the County Court for an injunction even outside court hours, but this is not possible in the Magistrates' Court which can only deal with applications during court time.

An emergency order will only be temporary. In the County Court, it will last until the earliest possible date when the whole case can be considered in full with an opportunity for your husband to have his say. An order of the Magistrates' Court made in an emergency can only last for a maximum of 28 days, even if there has not been an opportunity for a full investigation of the case before then. However, you can apply for it to be renewed at the end of the 28 day period.

The time actually taken to obtain an order, either in an emergency or in the normal way, will depend on all the circumstances not only what your case involves but also how busy the court is. It is sometimes possible to consult your solicitor in the morning and to have obtained a court order by the end of the day. On the other hand, if you are applying by routine procedure, it may take a week, or, in some cases, considerably more time before you have your order.

If you are really frightened of what your spouse might do, do make this clear to your solicitor – he does not necessarily know your spouse personally and, unless you tell him, he may not appreciate how much you need the court's protection.

Undertakings to the court

If you have made an application to the County Court, and your husband is willing to promise that he will not molest you or will move out of the house within a certain length of time (whatever it is you require), he may give the court what is known as an 'undertaking'. This is a formal promise to the court and is equivalent to an injunction. It will give you exactly the same protection as an injunction and if your husband breaks the promise, he is liable to exactly the same penalties as if he had broken the terms of an injunction.

Which court should I choose?

It really depends on the sort of order you need, whether you have already started divorce proceedings, how quickly you need help, whether you need legal aid to pay for the proceedings, how busy your local courts are etc. Your solicitor will make the decision for you. If, however, you have already started divorce proceedings, there will be no choice but to make your application to the Divorce County Court. Furthermore, you will also have to go to the County Court if you need protection from anti-social behaviour other than violence or threats of violence or if you need help outside court hours.

Enforcing the court's order

In many cases, the fact that the court has made an order will be enough to resolve the situation between you and your husband because he will comply with whatever the court decides. However, things are not quite so simple if your husband fails to obey the order, for instance if he does not move out of the house as he was ordered to do so or he continues to use violence towards you or to molest you in some other way.

Your next step depends on whether you were granted a *power of arrest* with the court order. This is a special order entitling the police to arrest your spouse straight away if he breaks the court order. If the court makes an order prohibiting your spouse from using violence towards you or a child of the family or excluding him from the home, and it is satisfied that he has already injured you or a child of the family and is likely to do so again, it can grant a power of arrest. You cannot expect the court to do this as a matter of course – the court does not look upon a power of arrest as a routine remedy and will be reluctant to grant one when you first obtain your order unless your case is particularly serious. However, if you have to go back at a later stage to the court because your husband has persistently disobeyed the order, you may well be able to get a power of arrest then. The power will normally last for up to three months, although you can apply to have it extended after that time.

If a power of arrest is granted with your order, and your husband breaks the court's order by using violence towards you or the child or by entering the house or the surrounding area after he has been excluded, you should contact your local police station. A police constable can then arrest your husband at once. If this happens he will be kept in custody and brought before the court (normally within 24 hours). Contact your solicitor as soon as possible after the incident so that he is aware of what is happening and can look after your interests. It is the responsibility of the police to arrange for your husband to be taken to court, but you will almost certainly have to give evidence to the Judge or Magistrates about what happened.

The court will have to decide what should be done about your husband's conduct. It can send him immediately to prison for whatever period it thinks appropriate. However, this is unlikely to happen if it is the first time he has broken the injunction or order, as imprisonment is usually reserved as something of a last resort for people who have persistently disobeyed the court's orders. Alternatively, the court can fine your husband.

There are often other, more constructive, courses of action open to the court instead of fines and imprisonment. For example, the court may decide to modify its original order in the light of what has happened, for instance, suppose that your husband has failed to comply with an order prohibiting him from molesting you because he simply cannot keep his temper when he is in contact with you – the court could, in these circumstances, modify its original order to exclude your husband from the home so that you have no further contact with each other. Another alternative would be for the court to put off the hearing for some time to give your husband one more chance to comply with the original order.

If you are not granted a power of arrest, it is up to you, with your solicitor's help, to take steps to bring your husband back to court if he breaks the order so that the court can decide what is to be done. Once you have brought the matter back before the court, the court has the same powers over your husband as it does where he is brought before it by means of a power of arrest.

The proceedings described so far in this chapter are 'civil' proceedings, in other words, they do not involve a criminal prosecution. If your spouse assaults you or damages your property, he will have committed a criminal offence just as he would if he behaved in this way to any other person. You can therefore call the police if something of this kind occurs (even if you do not have a power of arrest with your order) but you may well find that they are reluctant to interfere, without the backing of a power of arrest. Nevertheless, they may be prepared to come out to the incident and try to calm things down. They may sometimes even take criminal proceedings against your spouse depending on the particular circumstances of your case. If you are dissatisfied that the police are not prosecuting your husband, you may be able to bring a criminal prosecution against him yourself. This could result in his being sentenced to imprisonment. However, you are not recommended to do this. It really only deals with what is past, and gives you no guarantee that you will be protected in the future. Furthermore, you would be expected to meet the cost of the case out of your own pocket, whereas with civil proceedings you may well be eligible for Legal Aid.

Does the court's order have an effect on your own or your spouse's rights to your house?

Orders excluding your spouse from the home have no effect on the question of who owns the house. If your husband is the owner of the house but is ordered to leave for a period of time, he still owns the property even though he is temporarily prevented from enjoying the rights that an owner normally has.

The question of who should own and live in the house in the long term will be dealt with when the court considers what should be done about your property and finances in the long term, after the divorce.

Paying for your application

If you are eligible financially for Legal Aid, it may well be available to you to assist with the cost of your solicitor's advice and help in relation to an application for personal protection or in relation to your occupation of the house. This is the case, whether you are making or defending the application.

PART 4: THE CHILDREN

14 The Children: General Advice

There is no escaping the fact that even the most straightforward divorce will have some effect on your children. It inevitably brings with it a complete change in lifestyle for the whole family, to which it will take some time for you all to grow accustomed. Children are often very conservative by nature and can find it particularly difficult to accept that family life as they used to know it, has now gone for good. At times you may be tempted to wish that you had stayed together for the sake of the children and never embarked on a divorce at all. Nevertheless, if your marriage has completely broken down, divorce is often the most sensible solution, and, if you find the whole process rather discouraging at times, you should bear in mind that the children may have been caused a great deal more distress in the long run if you had gone on living together in a state of constant friction.

Once you have decided on divorce, the best you can do for the children is to try to make the process as painless as possible for them. This chapter attempts to give you some idea of how problems that arise in relation to the children can be resolved. Every family reacts differently to stress and no one can warn you of all the difficulties with which you may have to cope. It would certainly be presumptuous to try to tell you how to tackle every aspect of the situation with your own family. Nevertheless, there are some problems that seem to crop up over and over again and, as well as explaining the legal side of things, this chapter and the following two chapters try to offer some general advice to help you overcome or avoid difficulties that may arise.

Nothing that is suggested as general advice is in any way an 'expert opinion' on how to help children to cope with divorce – it is simply a mixture of the conclusions drawn from meeting families involved in divorce proceedings and common sense. Though sometimes it may seem like the counsel of perfection, if you bear the advice in mind, I hope you may at least find that it helps you to deal with the situations with which you are faced.

If you experience serious difficulties with your children (other than of a legal nature) you are urged to seek expert help from those qualified to deal with such problems. You should be able to find out who would be most suitable by discussing the matter with your doctor or the child's teacher. With children of school age, it is usually a good idea to keep in contact with the child's school anyway and to ask his teacher to tell you if he or she shows any signs at school of being disturbed over the divorce.

GENERAL ADVICE

1. Keeping a united front!

In the course of the divorce you will have to make a large number of decisions with your spouse over the future of the children. They will range from the most major decision – where the child is going to live when you separate – to decisions over access arrangements, education and religion, etc.

However much you may fight over each decision in private, you should do your utmost not to let the children become aware of this. Even very young children sense surprisingly quickly that there is a dispute going on between their parents over their future and they often find it very distressing. It is generally easier for children to accept decisions made for them if they feel that both parents are in agreement. If they sense a serious difference of opinion, they may start taking sides, or may feel very reluctant to accept what has been decided for fear of hurting the parent who did not fully agree with the decision.

If there has to be a court hearing over any questions relating to the children, it will be almost impossible to hide your differences of opinion from the children. It is far better for all concerned, therefore, if you can reach agreement over all the decisions you have to make jointly and thus avoid the need for a court to investigate and impose its judgments on the whole family.

2. The importance of giving careful thought to every decision that you make

Every decision that you make about the lives of your children is worthy of very careful consideration. It is easy, when you are feeling the strain of a divorce, to make rash and emotional decisions which you will later come to regret. So, before you come to any final conclusions on a problem, make sure that you have truly found the solution that is *best for your child*, even if it is not necessarily what you feel will bring you the most happiness.

If you feel that the children should know what is going on and what decisions have been made on their behalf, it will help them if you make sure that you can explain the situation to them in a way that they will understand and be able to accept, so it is often a good idea to sit down quietly first and consider how you are going to approach a particular matter with them.

Before you involve any of the children in any of the actual decision making, you should be absolutely sure that it is right for the particular child to be brought into discussions in this way. Whereas older children may have very clear views about a matter that they would welcome an opportunity to make known, younger children may be upset if you ask them what their feelings are and then their wishes have to be over-ruled.

3. Your attitude to the other parent

It is very tempting, when you are going through the process of a divorce, often feeling lonely and vulnerable, to try to get all your friends and relations on your side. Many people understandably also become anxious about losing the affection of their child to the other parent and, in an attempt to prevent this, sometimes start to run down the other parent in front of the child and to try to discourage the child from seeing him or her.

Once you are divorced and you are hoping to make a fresh start in life, your first reaction may well be to sever all your connections with your former spouse. However, if the children are to go on seeing him or her you will not be able to cut yourself off completely and you may find that you resent this.

It is only in very exceptional circumstances that the court will permit a clean break between the children and their other parent to take place, if that parent wants to go on seeing the children. You will make life much easier and happier for yourself and the children if you encourage contact between the children and their other parent and take great care not to try to turn the children against him or her and to keep any bad feelings that you may have about the whole subject strictly to yourself. You will probably find that as the children grow older, they will be very grateful to you for maintaining as normal a relationship with the other parent for them as is possible in the circumstances, whereas children who have been discouraged from seeing their other parent may grow up to resent this and sometimes even turn against the parent responsible.

4. Coping with a reaction against you

When one parent looks after the day to day needs of the child and the other parent only sees the child for short periods, the other parent naturally wants (and can often afford) to give the child treats and to spoil him when he sees him, whereas the parent with full time responsibility for the child has to maintain standards, keep within a tight budget and be responsible for discipline where necessary. Children do not always realise the reason why it may seem to be so much fun to be with the other parent. As a result, they sometimes make hurtful remarks to the parent who is responsible for their day to day care. There is no easy way round this and if you are the parent who has the privilege of the full time care of the child you may find that you have to put up with attempts by the child to play one parent off against the other, or with comments from the child such as 'I want to live with Daddy because he gives me sweets/takes me for a ride in his car/lets me play in the park . . .' or 'I'll tell Dad if you don't let me do such and such and he will let me come to live with him'. Behaviour of this kind, although it can be very upsetting for you, often does not mean very much; it is certainly very unlikely to mean that the child really does not want to go on living with you any more.

As the 'other parent' you can, of course, ease the situation by trying not to spoil the child when you see him, however tempting it might be, and making an effort not to say anything in front of the child that may undermine your ex-spouse's authority.

If you feel that you need moral support, or help, over your children, you may find it useful to contact an organisation that offers this type of assistance. You will find one or two suggestions in Chapter 27 about how to get in touch with an organisation suited to your needs.

15
Custody of the Children

Once you (or your spouse) have started divorce proceedings, you can ask the Divorce Court to make orders as to the custody, access and education of any of the children of your family who are under 18. If you encounter difficulties before divorce proceedings are commenced you can ask the Magistrates' Court or County Court to step in at once and decide issues of custody and access for you. Your solicitor will advise you as to your rights in other courts.

You should not confuse the Divorce Court's powers to decide issues of custody, access and education with the duty that it has to investigate and approve the arrangements that you have made for the children before finalising your divorce (see Chapter 10).

1. What is meant by 'custody' and 'access'?

'Custody' is a difficult word to define – even the courts do not entirely agree over what it means! In many cases, it is used to refer to the right of a parent to have his child living with him and to look after that child from day to day. This right is often also described as the right to have 'care and control' of the child. It used to be thought that the parent with custody also had the right to make most of the major decisions in the child's life without even consulting the other parent, for example decisions over the child's religion and education. However, recently the courts have stressed that neither parent has an *absolute* right to make decisions of this kind alone if the other parent has views on the matter.

There are three different types of custody order that the courts can make:

a) Custody to one parent: by far the most common order is a simple custody order whereby the court orders that one of the parents is to have custody and says nothing about who is to have care and control of the child. This means that the parent with the custody of the child will also be responsible for his everyday care and control and will have to make all the routine decisions that have to be made for him. When it comes to major decisions, it may well turn out that the parent with custody also makes these, but the other parent will have the right to raise any objections that he or she has. As you will see later in the chapter, once a custody order has been made, the freedom of either parent to make certain decisions is restricted, for example limitations are placed on the parent's right to have the child known by another surname.

Despite the fact that more and more fathers are becoming actively involved in the care of their children these days, it is still more common for a mother to be awarded custody of the children after a divorce and, when dealing with matters arising after the court order, this chapter is written as if the court had ordered that the mother should have custody. However, the same principles apply equally where a father has custody.

b) Joint custody: in a situation where the parents appear to be able to co-operate with each other and make decisions jointly, the court may make a joint custody order. When such an order is made, the custody of the child is given to both parents but the court specifically declares which of them is to have care and control of the child. Any major decisions that have to be made should be made by the parents jointly, although the parent with care and control will obviously have to be solely responsible for much of the routine organisation of the child's life, for example, deciding what time the child should go to bed, when he should do his homework, and, as he gets older, what time he should come in at night.

c) Custody to one parent and care and control to the other: this order has few advantages and is rarely made.

'Access' is normally taken to mean the right of a parent who does not have care and control of his child to see the child from time to time. In fact, the courts look upon access as the right of the *child*, rather than of the parent, which means that they approach every decision that has to be made about access by asking what is best for the child rather than what the parent would like.

2. When will the court make a custody order in a normal divorce case?

(a) *If you are not agreed over custody*

If you are not agreed over the question of custody, there will be no alternative but to ask the court to decide the issue for you. Although every attempt will be made to settle the matter as quickly as possible, there may be a delay before the court is able to give the matter full consideration and you may not obtain a final decision until some time after decree nisi of divorce has been granted.

If you come up against problems that cannot wait and you need urgent help, you can ask the Divorce Court to make a temporary custody order at any time after divorce proceedings are commenced. Unless the court is in possession of the full facts in relation to your case, however, the order will only be designed to tide you over until a proper investigation of your circumstances can take place; it will be called an 'interim custody order'.

It might be appropriate to apply for an interim order if, for example, the children are in the care of the other parent who will not let you take over and you are seriously worried about the standard of care they are receiving. However, in most cases you will find that the Judge will be very reluctant to interfere at all with the existing arrangements until he is in a position to make a long term decision about custody, unless it is absolutely necessary to do so. Your solicitor will be able to advise you whether it is worth applying to the court for an interim order or whether you should simply press on with your application for a full custody order as quickly as possible.

If you are in dispute over the children, it is important to take advice from a solicitor straight away. Children soon settle into a home and a routine and the longer they spend in the care of one parent, the less likely the court is to alter the arrangement to transfer the custody to the other parent, however good his case for custody may be.

(b) *If you are agreed over custody*

If you are agreed over custody, the court can normally make an order in favour of the appropriate parent when it considers the arrangements proposed for the children after pronouncement of decree nisi (see Chapter 10).

Even if the prospect of reaching agreement seems bleak at the outset, you may find that you ultimately manage to resolve your differences without the help of the court. If the court has been aware that you could not agree over custody, you will not automatically have been given an appointment with the Judge for the consideration of the arrangements for the children. Therefore, as soon as you reach agreement, you will have to notify the court of this and ask for an appointment to be fixed for you. When you attend the appointment, you will need to satisfy the Judge that you really have resolved the question of custody before he will make the custody order you require. The easiest way to do this is often for both you and the respondent to attend the hearing so that you can each confirm the agreement to him. If the Judge then feels it is appropriate, he will make a custody order in the agreed terms as well as considering the arrangements that you propose generally for the children.

3. Preparing for a court hearing to decide who is to have custody

The court needs to be fully informed about yourselves, the children and the arrangements you are proposing for custody, before it can make any decision as to who should look after the children. Both parents are often required to file affidavits with the court setting out their proposals for the future care of the children. When he has discussed your case thoroughly with you, your solicitor should ensure that an affidavit is prepared for you if this is necessary. Try to raise all your worries about the case, particularly any doubts you may have over the standard of care that the other parent would be likely to provide for the children, before he prepares the affidavit so that he can decide whether they should be mentioned in it or not. Remember that your solicitor is not familiar with your family life and will not necessarily be able to ask you about everything that could help your case, so be ready to volunteer any information that you think is important. On the other hand, do not be surprised if your solicitor does not include all the things you have told him in your affidavit – he will only deal with matters that he feels will influence the judgment of the court and you should be prepared to accept his advice on this. When your affidavit has been prepared, you will be required to check through it carefully before you swear to the truth of the contents. If you feel that any facts are misstated in the affidavit or that it does not represent your views properly, say so before you swear it so that it can be amended. If the other parent files an affidavit with the court, your solicitor will be provided with a copy of it and you will be able to make your comments on what has been said.

Tell your solicitor well in advance of any friends, relatives or independent people who you feel may be able to be witnesses in support of your case. If possible, you should tell your solicitor whether these people would be willing to come to court to speak for you if necessary – you may find that although people are very much on your side, they are not prepared to be drawn into a dispute between you and your spouse, especially if it would involve them in attending court. Your solicitor will be able to interview any witnesses that he feels may support your case and decide whether they should be asked to give evidence for you. If you have formed a new relationship with someone who is going to help you with the children or who is likely to be in contact with them regularly, or if you are intending to rely on a relative or friend for a substantial amount of help, you should inform your solicitor.

Although some of your witnesses may be able to give their evidence in writing in affidavits others may have to attend court if your spouse requests it. Furthermore the court will normally expect to hear oral evidence at the hearing from anyone who is going to be closely associated with the children so that it can assess the sort of person he or she is and ensure that he or she is suitable to be in contact with them. There is no need to worry if there is nobody who you feel would make a valuable witness for you. This frequently happens. In a lot of cases, your own evidence is all that really counts.

The court will almost always ask for an independent report about your case to assist it with its decision. This report will be prepared by a welfare officer, who will be a probation officer or social worker who is experienced in dealing with custody cases. He has a duty to investigate the circumstances of your case, in whatever way he thinks best. He will normally want to visit your home and the home that the other parent is offering the children, and to discuss with both of you individually, the family history, the proposals you are making for the children, and any worries that you have about the care that the other parent would provide for the children if he or she were to get custody. It will help the welfare officer if you discuss matters freely with him and co-operate with him as far as possible. It is also in your own interests to do so, because the welfare officer often includes a recommendation in his report to the court, as to who should have custody of the children and he will obviously not feel well disposed towards a parent who has been bad tempered and obstructive. He will probably also want to meet anyone else who is going to be in close contact with the children.

Most welfare officers like to meet all but the youngest children concerned in the case. It frequently helps them to see the children both in your company and on their own. You do not need to worry that the welfare officer will upset the children in any way; he will be very careful not to question them directly about the custody issue unless they are obviously old enough to have clear views about it. In the case of younger children, the welfare officer may simply want to play with the children and chat to them generally. He will probably also make a number of other enquiries (for example, he may interview the child's teacher to see how he is getting on at school) but the exact nature of these enquiries will vary according to the circumstances of your case and the practice of the particular officer.

Once the welfare officer has collected all the information he requires, he will prepare a written report for the court, telling the court what he has found out about the case, and making any recommendations about custody (and access) that he thinks are appropriate. You are entitled to see the report. Your solicitor will normally obtain a copy at or before the hearing of the case and go through it with you to check that you agree with the contents.

4. The court hearing

When all the evidence is ready, the next step is the hearing itself which will take place in front of the Judge. Although this may well be the first time you have attended court, there is no need to be anxious about the hearing. Your solicitor, and possibly also a barrister, will be there to represent you and they will make sure that you know what to do throughout the proceedings. The hearing is held in chambers, in private, and will be fairly informal. Only people who are directly concerned with the case will be allowed to be present – no members of the general public will be admitted. Sometimes the hearing will take place in the Judge's private room; in other cases, the hearing will take place in the court room itself. The choice of venue will depend on a variety of factors including the number of people involved in the case and the preference of the Judge who is going to hear the case. You may be asked to attend court rather earlier than the time fixed for your hearing so that you have time to discuss everything with your solicitor or barrister. Any witnesses that you may have will also be notified to attend court in good time for the hearing.

When the Judge is ready to hear your case, you will be told where to sit whilst your solicitor (or barrister) or your spouse's solicitor (or barrister) explains to the Judge what the case is all about. Then either you or your spouse will be required to give evidence first. When your turn comes to give evidence, you will be asked to take an oath swearing that the evidence you give will be the truth. If, for religious reasons, you are not prepared to swear an oath on the Bible, mention this to your solicitor before the hearing starts so that he can see that alternative arrangements are made for you. When you give your evidence, you will be asked questions about the case to make sure that you cover all the matters about which the Judge needs to know. Be careful to listen to the questions that are asked of you and to give your answers as concisely as possible, in a clear, loud voice. You will see that people are making notes of what you say, so do not be tempted to rattle off your answers at great speed. Do not be afraid to ask for a question to be repeated or rephrased if you did not understand it. If you find that your mind goes blank when you are asked a question, it is best simply to explain what has happened; you will find that most Judges and lawyers are very sympathetic about this type of problem – it has probably happened to *them* once or twice in their careers. Any witnesses who have attended court will be given the opportunity to give their evidence during the proceedings, and if the welfare officer is present at court, he will sometimes be called upon to give evidence also.

Parents often wonder whether the children concerned will have to be brought to court for the custody hearing. It is rarely appropriate for a child to give evidence as a witness for one or the other parent in a custody dispute – it can be very upsetting for the child to be required to do so. However, the Judge can see the child in his room, in private, and have a chat with him if he feels this will help him to decide the custody issue. There is no general rule about when a Judge will want to do this. It depends on the circumstances of the case, the age of the child and the attitude of the Judge concerned. A few Judges like to see children of about school age upwards, others prefer only to see teenage children, and some seldom wish to see any children whatever their age. Your solicitor will be able to tell you whether it is necessary for the children to attend in your case. If they do have to come to court, you can rest assured that every effort will be made to ensure that they are not kept waiting at court for longer than is absolutely necessary, and that their meeting with the Judge will be very informal and usually very brief.

When all the evidence has been put before the court, the solicitors (or barristers) will have the opportunity to address the Judge in support of your respective applications. The Judge will then make his decision. Once you know the outcome of the case, you should always have a word with your solicitor before leaving court. There are often matters that arise from the decision to be sorted out, for example, if the children are to move from one parent to live with the other, arrangements will have to be made about when this will take place, and in many cases there will be questions to be resolved about access.

5. Later changes in the custody order

The order that the court makes after a full consideration of the evidence is usually designed to be a long term arrangement. However a custody order is never absolutely final and can always be altered if circumstances should change to make this necessary. This does not mean that a parent who is dissatisfied with the court's order can simply return to court a month later and ask for the decision to be changed. But it does mean that if, in the future, the parent who does not have custody has any serious worries about the way in which the children are being brought up, he has the right to re-open the whole question of custody. There are numerous reasons why the court might be prepared to alter the existing custody order, for example, if the parent who has custody is wrongly preventing the other parent from seeing the children, or if she has become unsuitable to care for the children since the original court hearing. There may also be straightforward reasons for varying the original order, for example, the child may have expressed a firm wish to live with the other parent and both parents may agree that this wish should be respected.

You should not think that it is easy to persuade the court to alter an existing custody order, unless both parties agree that this should be done. Judges generally feel that once a child has settled into a routine with one parent, there has to be a very strong reason to justify putting the child through all the upheaval that a variation of the custody order would cause.

6. How does a court decide who is to have custody?

When it makes its decision as to who is to have custody of a child, the court is always guided by the same principle – that it should do whatever is best for the child.

No two cases will ever be the same so there can be no hard and fast rules about when a mother should have custody and when the father has the better claim. All the circumstances of the case will be considered by the Judge before he makes his decision. You will have to turn to your solicitor for advice on the probable outcome of your own case, but you may find it helpful to know what sort of factors the Judge will be likely to bear in mind when resolving the custody issue.

(a) *The physical well-being of the child*
Most families nowadays are able to provide housing for their children, and state benefits generally ensure that provision can be made for the children's basic needs of food and clothing. The court will compare the standard of accommodation offered by each parent and assess how suitable it is for the child. For example, the Judge might have to decide whether it would be better for a child to live with its mother in a high-rise flat in the centre of a big town or with its father in a detached house with a garden in the suburbs. At first sight the answer may seem to be obvious, but in fact, although it will be taken into consideration, the greater material prosperity and pleasanter surroundings offered by one parent will not normally be the decisive factor in a case. In any event, the courts are often able to go some way towards equalising the differences between the parents in this respect when they deal with the family property and maintenance after the divorce. (See Chapter 21.)

What is likely to be more important is the day to day care that each parent is likely to provide for the child. The Judge will need to be sure that the child will be fed properly, that the home will be kept clean, that adequate clothing will be provided and that suitable babysitting arrangements will always be made for the child who is young enough still to require this. If there is any serious doubt as to whether one of the parents will live up to the required standards, that parent will be at a disadvantage in the custody proceedings. If the evidence suggests that a parent will actually neglect or ill treat the child in some way, that parent will be very unlikely to get custody.

Fortunately, in most custody disputes, it is quite clear that both parents will provide first class care for the child and the court has no need even to consider this aspect of the case.

(b) *The special problems faced by the working parent*
For the parent who goes out to work, there will be a special problem of who is to look after the children when he or she cannot be there. Many couples nowadays both work, even after they have a family. Both would have to find a substitute to look after the children after school, or if they are ill, or in school holidays etc. The court will need to have details of the outside help that each parent proposes to use. The court will normally be

more inclined to give custody to a parent who will be relying on someone the children know and like, than to a parent who has to rely on a total stranger.

Sometimes the court is faced with a situation where only one of the parents (usually the father goes out to work, whereas the other can be at home full time to look after the children. In such a case, of course, only the father will have to rely on outside help with the children and he is bound to be at a disadvantage in applying for custody because (where both parents are equally suitable in all other respects) the court will obviously be more inclined to grant custody to the mother who can be there whenever the children need her.

(c) *Mother or father?*
Neither parent has a better right to custody than the other; it all depends on the circumstances of the case. However, as a general rule, the mother has a better chance of getting custody of young children, and particularly of babies, than the father. Even now, when fathers do so much more towards the daily care of their children, it is very hard to displace the established attitude that it is a mother's job to stay at home and look after the children and a father's to go out to work.

(d) *The behaviour of both parents*
The court will not be prepared to investigate who has caused the breakdown of the marriage and how one parent has behaved towards the other, unless this behaviour has affected the children in some way or is likely to make the 'guilty' party unsuitable to look after them in the future. It is generally accepted that when a marriage is breaking down, there is inevitably a certain amount of unpleasant behaviour (sometimes even violence) on the part of both spouses, which will not usually affect their capacity to be very good parents. On the other hand, there are cases where a parent has behaved in a way that does directly affect his or her suitability as a parent.

Perhaps an example will most easily help you to appreciate how the courts approach the matter: let us suppose that Mrs. A falls for Mr. B during her marriage to Mr. A. She continues to take perfectly good care of her three children but, from time to time, she sees Mr. B whilst the children are at school and has sexual intercourse with him. This fact alone does not make her unsuitable to be a mother in any way. But, suppose that after the divorce, she starts to go out at night, five or six times a week, leaving the children in the care of young babysitters. Each week or so she brings home a different boyfriend who sleeps with her in her bed. Behaviour of this kind may have a serious effect on the children and would affect Mrs. A's suitability as a parent. Whereas the court would not wish to hear any evidence in the custody dispute about Mrs. A's association with Mr. B, it might well consider evidence of the second kind, of promiscuity and irresponsible behaviour, vital to its decision.

In another example, as their marriage deteriorates, Mr. and Mrs. C start to have frequent arguments. On one or two occasions, in the course of particularly heated arguments, Mr. C loses his temper and slaps Mrs. C across the face. She is not seriously hurt. The children are asleep in bed at the time and do not know anything about this. This lapse on the part of Mr. C would not be likely to influence the court's decision in any way. On the other hand, if Mr. C had been repeatedly violent towards his wife during the marriage, and had even beaten her up seriously in front of the children several times, this would weigh heavily against him in a custody dispute.

It is not only the behaviour of the parents towards each other that can be important. There are other aspects of the behaviour of a spouse that would also be likely to have a bearing on the court's decision. For example, it may be very important for the court to know that one spouse is a practising homosexual, or is involved in prostitution, or has an unending criminal record, or a recurrent history of serious mental illness, or belongs to an extreme religious sect.

(e) *The family ties*

In some families there is a particularly strong bond between a child and one of his parents. The court will take this into account in deciding who is to have custody. Even if the child does not show any particular attachment to either parent, the court will need to be sure that the parent who gets custody will provide the children with the love, understanding, discipline and moral support that they will need as they grow up.

There is usually a close relationship between brothers and sisters, and the court is extremely reluctant to split them up between parents, although if there are very special circumstances that really justify such a course, the court can order that some of the children go to the mother and some to the father.

(f) *The need for stability in the child's life*
Children do not normally react well to change. Their lives are inevitably disrupted once when the marriage breaks down, and Judges are always very anxious to make sure that once they have started to get over this, they are subjected to as little change as possible in their daily lives. This means that the parent who has the day to day care of the children at the time when the custody application is heard will have a considerable advantage over the other parent, particularly if the children have become settled with him or her for any length of time. If it would be right to move the child, the court will do so, but it will need to be given strong reasons why this is necessary.

(g) *The child's own view*
The Judge may get to know the child's wishes about custody (if he has expressed any) from the welfare report or from interviewing the child himself. The older the child becomes, the more difficult it is to force him to accept a decision about custody with which he does not agree. So, if older children have clear views about where they would like to live, this will be a factor that will probably influence the Judge's decision quite heavily. On the other hand the Judge will always bear in mind that a child of any age may have been influenced by one of his parents or may not be voicing his true feelings for some other reason. The younger the child is, the less attention the court will pay to his own wishes about custody.

(h) *The attitude of each parent towards the other*
It is considered very important, in most cases, that the child should continue to have a good relationship with the parent who does not have custody and to see that parent regularly. It will count against a parent if he or she attempts to spoil this relationship in any way, for example by making derogatory remarks about the other parent in front of the child or discouraging or preventing access visits. In extreme cases, if a parent behaves particularly badly in this respect, it can be the deciding factor in the custody case.

(i) *The welfare report*
The welfare report is very important. If the welfare officer makes a recommendation in respect of custody, this will carry a very great deal of weight, although it is not the last word on the matter – that rests with the Judge.

7. Some points to watch out for after the custody order

(a) *Changing your child's surname*

If you remarry after your divorce or revert to your maiden name, you may want the children of whom you have custody to be known by your new surname, to save embarrassment and inconvenience. However, the law restricts your right to change your child's surname without the consent of the other parent or the permission of the court. If you look at the court order awarding you custody, you will see that it expressly forbids you to take any step that would result in the children being known by a different surname (for example registering them at school under your new surname) before they reach the age of 18, unless you obtain either the other parent's consent or the court's leave. If the other parent will not consent and you have to apply to the court for permission, you will have to convince the court that it is in the child's best interests to be known by a new surname.

This restriction does not affect the right of a daughter who marries before she is 18 to take her husband's surname.

(b) *Taking the child abroad*

The English courts can generally enforce the orders that they make only against people who are either present within England and Wales or who have property here. This means that once a parent removes a child from England and Wales, the court no longer has any control over what happens to that child and is virtually powerless to step in and safeguard the child if necessary. You may have read in the newspapers of cases where one parent takes the child abroad without the knowledge of the other parent who has legal custody – often you will have seen that there is nothing at all that can be done about this in this country, except appeal publicly to the parent to return the child.

To prevent this type of problem from arising, custody orders restrict the right of either parent to take the child out of England and Wales:–

1) Temporary trips outside England and Wales:–

Custody orders normally provide that, until he is 18, a child may not be taken outside England and Wales without the court's permission. However this does not mean that you need to make an application for permission from the court every time you want to go away for a holiday. You will usually be able to give a 'once-and-for-all', general written undertaking to the court promising to return the child to England and Wales when called upon to do so. Provided that you then obtain the written consent of the child's other parent whenever you wish to take the child out of the country, you will be allowed to do so for whatever period is specified in that written consent.

2) Taking a child abroad permanently:-
It is a quite different and serious step to take a child abroad permanently. It will usually mean that contact with the other parent is restricted or that it may have to cease altogether. It also means that the English courts may no longer have any control over the child's upbringing. You are therefore required to obtain the court's permission before you take a child out of England and Wales permanently. Permission is not granted automatically by any means. The court will consider what is in the child's best interests, bearing in mind that it may not be fair to restrict your own freedom too much. You will usually be required, if you are given leave by the court, to undertake to return the child to England and Wales should this ever become necessary.

If you are genuinely afraid that the other parent may try to take the child abroad without proper authority, contact your solicitor *at once* so that he can take steps to prevent this. There is no need to wait until a custody order has been made or even until divorce proceedings have commenced. There are preventive measures that can be taken at any stage, even during your marriage, if necessary.

16
Access

If you do not have care and control of your child, you are entitled to expect reasonable access. What is reasonable varies according to the circumstances of your case - access visits can range from long periods (perhaps even the whole of the school holidays) staying with the other parent, to an hour or two with him in the park.

The court will expect you to be able to agree over what access is reasonable in your case. If you cannot do so, the court will decide the matter for you by defining when access should take place. However, although this service is available, it is essential that you try to sort out as many of the arrangements as possible between yourselves. You can expect very short shrift from the court if you come along asking it to fix every last detail of every access visit for years to come. Do try to remain amicable over access. If you do, you will make things so much easier for your children. Remember that although you have fallen out with each other, the children are probably still very much attached to each of you and it is most important for them to maintain contact with both of you. An access visit can seem quite artificial and strained enough to a child without its being preceded by endless arguments between his parents.

Some parents, after they are divorced, are mistakenly tempted to try to cut off all contact between the child and the other parent. This happens for a variety of reasons – frequently a mother will convince herself that this is the right thing to do because the father is a bad influence and upsets the child. However, the underlying reason may often be that she wants to make quite sure that she does not lose the child's love and affection to the other parent. What is more, she may still be feeling very hurt after the divorce and by preventing access she may have one way in which she can hit back at her ex-husband.

Rest assured it is only in quite exceptional cases, where there is strong evidence that it is not in the child's best interests to continue with access, that access will be prevented by the court when you want it to continue and are prepared to make efforts to see your child.

It may help to bear in mind the following points when deciding what access you think is reasonable in your case:

1. If you left it up to the court to decide what access should take place, the court would order whatever it thought was best for your child – you should use the same yardstick when agreeing your own arrangements.

2. Children who live with one parent and have access to the other inevitably have to divide their time between two separate lives. As they grow older, they will make friends in the area where they live and will no doubt want to participate in all sorts of activities, usually at weekends, such as sports matches and school outings. It can be disappointing for them and cause resentment if they always miss this type of activity because access visits have to take place on the day concerned. When fixing access arrangements you should take this into account;

for example, it may not be a good idea to arrange for your child to spend *every* weekend with you because this will prevent him from having a normal home life – it would probably be better for him to stay with you every other weekend, or perhaps three weekends out of four.

As well as making sure that your child does not miss too many things he would like to do with his friends wise parents remain flexible about access for other reasons. It is in the interests of both of you to do so as you will probably each want to take advantage of the flexibility of arrangements from time to time.

If your child tells you he wants to take part in the school fête on the Saturday when you would normally have access, for example, try to rearrange your access visit for another day; suppose that the mother wants to take the children for a fortnight's holiday – she might find it very helpful to rearrange access so that the holiday could be for an unbroken period; or if the father has to stay away on business when he would normally have had access, he will want to see the children at another time if possible. If access arrangements are to remain adaptable, both parents will have to be very co-operative.

3. Even if you have a flexible arrangement for access, try to fix the details of visits a reasonable time in advance and stick to them exactly. This may not always be possible (for example, one of you may be ill) but if you have to cancel a visit for any reason, try to let the other parent know as soon as possible. Nothing is more upsetting for children than to be in a state of perpetual uncertainty over access and it is particularly soul destroying for them to be all ready for a day out with their father or mother, who simply fails to turn up without giving any reason, or who cancels arrangements at the last minute.

4. When you only see your child for access, it is very tempting to spoil him and to let him get away with 'murder'. A little bit of indulgence will probably do no harm at all but you do need to be careful that you do not undermine the other parent's authority in any way or make it difficult for the child to settle back into his everyday routine after access.

5. If your child has friends in your area with whom he would like to play on access visits, do not feel that he is obliged to spend the whole day with you. You are free to spend the day in whatever way suits both of you best.

6. Coping with the effects of an access visit may require some patience from the parent with custody. Even the best managed access visits can disrupt the child's home life and you can expect

him to be excited before access and often a little upset, perhaps even badly behaved, after access until he has settled down into his routine again. Do not be too quick to blame the other parent for this (or the child) – it may be inevitable.

Staying or visiting access?

(a) *Staying access*:– There will be no prospect of a court permitting you to have staying access unless you can provide satisfactory accommodation for your child when he stays with you. If you hope to have the child to stay for prolonged periods, you (or someone on your behalf) will have to be able to cope with everyday chores such as washing and ironing the child's clothes. Very young children are perhaps less likely to benefit from staying access than older children, and babies, especially, may not be able to be away from their mothers overnight. If your child genuinely does not want to stay away overnight, the court would be unlikely to order him to do so. In the early days after a divorce or after a custody order has been made, your child may need some time to settle down to his new life and it can sometimes be a good idea to let him have a period without staying access in which to find his feet. However there is usually no reason why regular access visits should not be arranged during this period so that the child can remain in close contact with you.

If staying access is arranged and is working well, it can often be increased to quite extensive periods, perhaps up to or exceeding half of each school holiday and one weekend in every two or three.

(b) *Visiting access*:– Staying access may not be a practical proposition for a variety of reasons. If so, you will have to content yourself with seeing the children during the day and returning them to their mother at night. This can pose something of a problem if you live some way away from the child – if you take the child home for the visit, the whole day will be spent travelling, whereas if you stay in the area all day, you risk the child becoming bored because it is a problem to find suitable entertainment. You should be careful to bear these difficulties in mind when you arrange the time and place where you will collect the child for access and when and where you will return him. Make sure that the 'pick-up point' that you arrange is convenient for both parents (bearing in mind the public transport available if either of you has to rely on this) and has somewhere where you can wait in comfort if the other parent is delayed. Obviously it will cause the least problems if you can pick the child up at his home. You need not come into contact with the other parent if she keeps an eye open for your arrival and sends the child out to you when you come. Punctuality is vital when collecting and returning the child – if you are late (or even unduly early) you will probably have to contend with an irate parent and a distraught child!

(c) *Supervised access*:– You may find that even short periods of access cause problems of one sort or another. It may help if you can arrange for a third party, perhaps a relative whom your child knows, to be present on a few occasions. On the other hand, it is not normally very successful to have both parents present during an access visit, because both you and your child will probably find it impossible to behave naturally.

If the court is worried about access, it can sometimes arrange for one or two access visits to be supervised by an independent person, for example a social worker, to make sure that everything is working out all right (see Chapter 17).

Do we need to make any firm arrangements for access at all?
If you live within easy reach of the children and they are old enough to make their own arrangements to come and see you, there is no reason why you should not leave it up to them to pop in and see you whenever they want rather than arranging for access visits at particular times.

Christmas Day and other special occasions
A lot of bad feeling can be caused over Christmas Day and other special occasions during the year. Christmas Day in particular is very special for both parents and children, and neither parent will want to be without the children on that day. If you live sufficiently close, you may be able to arrange for the children to spend part of the day with each of you. If this is not possible, the fairest way is usually for one parent to have the children on Christmas Day one year (and the other to see them on Christmas Eve or Boxing Day) and the other parent to have them for Christmas Day the next year. If any other days are particularly special for your family, for example birthdays, you could try to come to an arrangement to alternate these in a similar way. If you live close enough to each other, there should be no reason why you cannot arrange a meeting beween your child and his other parent so that he can have his birthday present from that parent personally on the day.

Asking the court to resolve disputes over access

If you are unable to reach agreement over access you can ask the court to settle the matter for you. It is sometimes convenient for the court to make an order defining access when it decides the custody issue; in other cases, a separate access hearing has to be arranged.

If a separate hearing is fixed, you will find that the procedure for preparing the case and at the court itself is much the same as for the custody hearing described in the preceding chapter. However, access problems can sometimes be dealt with by a Registrar rather than by a Judge. Whoever decides the case will probably require a welfare report to assist him, just as in a custody dispute.

Like a custody order, an access order is never final. Either parent can ask the court to reconsider the question if the circumstances warrant this. It is important to realise that even if the court does lay down fixed times for access, you can change these by agreement between you without referring the matter to the court. There is absolutely no reason why you should not arrange for more access to take place than the court order provides if you both agree. You cannot, however, either of you alter the times and places or the number of access visits fixed by the court if the other parent does *not* agree.

17 Supervision of the Arrangements for the Children

Supervision generally

Whenever the court makes an order in relation to custody or access, it can also order that the child concerned should be under the supervision of an independent person, usually a probation officer or social worker. This is not a routine order – the court will consider making a supervision order if one is recommended by the welfare report prepared for the court, or if the court itself has any worries about the welfare of the children.

Supervision can be helpful in all sorts of ways. It enables the court to make sure that the child is being properly cared for once it has made its order as to custody or access. It provides the parent with custody with the benefit of the moral support and advice of an experienced person in dealing with any difficulties that may arise over the child. It reassures the parent who does not have custody by the knowledge that someone else is keeping an eye on the child for him, even though he cannot be with him or her all the time himself. If problems are encountered over access arrangements it can be very helpful to both parents and the court to have an independent negotiator who can assist everybody to come to the best possible solution by agreement.

How much contact you will have with the supervisor will depend a lot on his or her practice and your own particular needs. Even if you have no regular arrangement to see your supervisor, however, you will be able to contact him or her if you come up against any particular problem with which you need help.

A supervision order does not usually have any time limit set upon it and can continue indefinitely until the child concerned reaches 18. On the other hand, the court can vary the order to take account of changes in circumstances, or discharge the order before it has run its course if it feels that it is no longer needed.

Supervised access

If there are extreme problems over access visits, it is sometimes possible for the court to arrange for a social worker or probation officer to be present during one or two periods of access to make sure everything runs smoothly. It can do this whether or not it also makes a general supervision order in relation to the child concerned.

Because most parents can only see their children for access outside normal office hours, it can be very difficult to arrange for supervised access without making unfair demands on the social worker or probation officer involved. Therefore the court will only order supervised access if neither of you can suggest an acceptable third person (for example an unbiased friend, or a godparent of the child) who could undertake to be present during a few access visits and if the social worker or probation officer is in a position to and agrees to help, and can arrange a suitable time and place for the visit.

PART 5: REACHING AGREEMENT ABOUT THE FUTURE

18 Coming to an Agreement over Arrangements for the Future

There are so many things that must be planned when you separate or get divorced – who is to live in the family home? Who is to pay the mortgage instalments, look after the children, meet the household bills, pay the rates, deal with the school fees?

Many people prefer to make their own arrangements for the future without involving the court. If you can come to an agreement over things yourselves, so much the better – you will both benefit from an amicable arrangement that cuts out the bickering and unpleasantness which often arises if you have to ask the court to sort out your affairs for you.

You may find it impossible to come to terms in the initial stages of separation and divorce and only manage to agree as the court hearing about your property and finances draws near. This chapter is not about that sort of agreement – if you are in that situation, you should refer to Chapter 21. This chapter deals with agreements that are made freely between you at an earlier stage, before the court has become involved in the financial side of things at all.

Considerations to bear in mind when making an agreement

1. WHAT SHOULD GO INTO THE AGREEMENT?

You can deal with all sorts of matters – your separation, maintenance for yourself and the children, payment of a more substantial lump sum of money by one of you to the other, details about the house (who is to live there, own it, pay the outgoings etc.), who is to look after the children, access to the children and so on. The exact contents of your agreement are up to the two of you. Generally, the more you can resolve in your agreement, the better. But do not be deterred from making an agreement about some matters, just because you cannot agree over everything.

2. WHY MAKE AN AGREEMENT?

You may wonder whether there is any point in making a formal agreement – perhaps you already have an informal arrangement that you have never really discussed but which seems to work reasonably well in practice, or perhaps you have agreed on things in discussion but never got round to writing anything down.

In fact, there are practical and tax advantages of making a formal arrangement, particularly when it come to financial matters:

a) *Financial aspects:* a voluntary arrangement is all very well, but have you considered that your wife may be finding it difficult to budget because she cannot be sure what she will receive by way of maintenance from you at the end of the week or month? Have you experienced difficulties in making yourself pay what you know your wife needs because you are hard up yourself and, because you are not bound to give her anything, is it too tempting to give her less than you promised, or nothing at all?

With a firm agreement, you know exactly what you have to pay and when, and you can budget for it. Your wife knows that she can rely on that sum at regular intervals. Furthermore you can claim tax relief for the payments that you make to your wife (though not the payments you make to or for the benefit of your children) whereas no tax relief is available for voluntary maintenance – see Chapter 22. You will probably find therefore, that you have more money in your pocket from which to provide for your family and yourself.

b) *Other aspects:* you may not feel it is so important to record other arrangements in a formal agreement, particularly if they are of the type that are best kept flexible, for example access arrangements. However, people do quite often like to make a formal agreement to separate, just to put things on a definite basis for the future. Others like to include everything that has been sorted out in the agreement just to tie up all the loose ends.

3. HOW DOES ONE GO ABOUT MAKING AN AGREEMENT?

Agreements should generally be in writing. Agreements by word of mouth only are not a good idea they can give rise to disputes between you in the future over exactly what was arranged, and, furthermore, an oral agreement may not necessarily be sufficient to enable you to get tax relief for maintenance payments that you have undertaken to pay (see Chapter 22).

Depending on what you have agreed, it may be possible for the agreement simply to be written out clearly, or it may be necessary for it to be embodied in a formal legal deed, signed and sealed in the presence of witnesses.

To make sure that your agreement will be binding and effective, it is important that you consult your solicitor. Take his advice on the terms of the agreement. He will make sure that the arrangement you have arrived at is fair and reasonable for you and that the written document that is drawn up really does represent what you both intended. It is usually preferable for each of you to take advice from a separate solicitor over the agreement so that neither of you feels aggrieved, when looking back on the agreement, because the solicitor's advice seemed to favour the other spouse.

4. WHAT THE AGREEMENT CANNOT DO.

a) The agreement you reach cannot prevent either of you from subsequently applying to court to have your financial position reviewed. Some people try to rule out the possibility of such an application by, for example, a term in the agreement that provides that the wife undertakes that, providing her husband pays her the maintenance agreed, she will never apply to the court for further maintenance or for any further share in the family property. Terms such as this have no effect whatsoever.

b) An agreement cannot make arrangements to cope with the situation *if* you separate at some date in the future. The law looks upon this as an encouragement to you to separate of which it disapproves as contrary to public policy. Nevertheless, this does not mean that you have to wait until you have actually separated before you make your agreement – you are quite free to make an agreement *on the occasion of your immediate* separation.

5. CAN THE AGREEMENT EVER BE MADE FINAL?

No arrangements that you make with regard to the children will be final, whatever you agree between the two of you. The court can always step in and change what you have agreed over custody, access and maintenance of the children, at the request of either of you.

If you agree to separate, the court cannot force you to live together again, so in a sense this part of your agreement is final. However, should you decide between you that you would like to give the marriage another try, there is no reason why you should not start to live together again, whatever your agreement says.

If you wish to do so, you *can* make your financial and property arrangements final in so far as they affect the two of you, provided (i) that your arrangements do not involve the payment of maintenance from one of you to the other and (ii) that you are prepared to enlist the help of the court.

Not all couples will want, or be able, to make final arrangements, but for example, a young couple with no children may prefer to make a clean break after their divorce and might arrange that they each take half of all their combined assets and that neither will make any claims on the other for maintenance in the future. Or an older wife whose children have left home and who is working part-time, might agree to accept all her husband's share in his family home as well as her own, and in return to release him from any obligation to maintain her in the future (as he would have had to do had she taken a smaller share of the family capital).

To make this type of arrangement final, you require a court order. What happens is that the court makes an order providing for all the matters upon which you have agreed and then dismisses all the other claims that either of you might have made on divorce. So, in the case of the young couple and the older wife, the court would dismiss each wife's claim to maintenance and would order that the couple's assets be divided up as they had agreed. The wives would lose their rights to claim maintenance ever again as soon as the court order was made.

6. TAX CONSIDERATIONS

It is important to have an eye to the tax position when you enter into any agreement over your property and income, particularly when it involves one of you in paying maintenance to the other or to a child of the family. You will find details of how your tax position is likely to be affected in Chapter 22. As you will see from that chapter, whatever arrangements you come to for yourselves, it is often a good idea to have your agreement over maintenance for the children embodied in a court order to get maximum tax relief.

Considerations whilst the agreement is in force

1. WHAT OBLIGATIONS DO YOU BOTH HAVE?
Whilst the agreement is in force, you are both bound by its terms. If either of you breaks the agreement, the other can take steps to have it enforced by the court. You should refer to Chapter 23 for the procedure whereby agreements can be enforced.

2. VARYING THE AGREEMENT
a) *If you both agree to the alteration:* there is no reason why you should not change the terms of your agreement in the future (for example to increase or decrease the amount of maintenance payable) if you both agree. It would be a good idea to check with your solicitor whether the variation needs to be put in a formal deed.

b) *If you do not agree:* the spouse seeking the change may be able to apply to the court for a new arrangement to be ordered. As you have seen, the court can always order a change in relation to arrangements for the children if it feels it is necessary to do so. As for financial arrangements for the two of you, unless you have made your arrangement final by a court order as described in paragraph 5 above, there may be two ways in which you could have it altered: (i) if your agreement is in writing and you can show that circumstances have changed since you made it so that it no longer makes fair financial provision for you, you can ask the court to step in and repair the deficiency in the agreement. For example, it might raise the amount of maintenance you are receiving under the agreement because your husband's salary has gone up substantially. It can even make provisions about finance where the original agreement only dealt with separation and did not mention money at all;

or (ii) if you are going through a divorce and you have not yet had your financial and property position dealt with by the court as part of the divorce proceedings, you can make an application for financial provision and property adjustment orders in the normal way (see Chapter 21) despite your agreement. However, when the court considers your application it will bear in mind the provisions of your agreement, and it will be an uphill (if not impossible) task to persuade the court to make orders that conflict with the terms of your agreement if circumstances have remained unchanged since you made it and you had independent legal advice at the time.

3. HOW LONG WILL THE AGREEMENT LAST?

There are a number of ways in which an agreement can come to an end:

a) *By agreement:* your agreement will terminate in accordance with any time limit that you fixed when you made it. For example, if you agreed that it would continue until your youngest living child reached 18, it will terminate on this event. Alternatively, you can agree after the agreement has been running for a while that it should come to an end. If you do so, it will terminate in accordance with this fresh agreement.

b) *By breach:* if one of you is guilty of a serious failure to observe the terms of the agreement, the other may be free to look upon the agreement as at an end, if he or she wishes to do so. Alternatively, he or she could apply to the court to enforce the agreement (see Chapter 23). It will not be enough that your spouse has simply failed to pay the maintenance he or she agreed to under the agreement on one or two occasions. But if the failure were to continue for a substantial period of time, this might release you from your obligations under the agreement. Your solicitor will advise you when this point is reached.

c) *By beginning to live together again:* if you start to live together again after you have made the agreement, this may or may not put an end to the agreement for good. It will depend on the way in which your agreement is drafted and what you intended to happen in such a situation. You should take your solicitor's advice as to whether it is necessary to make a new agreement if you subsequently separate again.

d) *By death or remarriage:* it may well be implied in the agreement, that no financial obligations will exist between you after the death of one of you. So, for example, an agreement for a husband to pay a wife weekly maintenance may cease when he dies so that his estate will have no liability to maintain the wife. It may also be implied that the payment of maintenance should cease if the payee remarries. Suppose, for instance, you agree to pay your wife £50 per week. A year later, she gets married again. Your obligation to maintain her may cease when she remarries.

PART 6: FINANCIAL ARRANGEMENTS

19 Preventing your Spouse from Running off with all the Family Assets

Normally, when a divorce takes place, the couple concerned decide between them what should happen to their house and other property after the divorce or, if they cannot agree, they refer the matter to the court for a decision as to who is to have what.

Sometimes, however, one spouse is not prepared to play by the rules, and when he realises that a divorce is inevitable, makes plans to dispose of all the family finance and property so that the other spouse cannot lay any claim to it. For example, a husband may decide to sell the house without his wife's consent and fritter away the proceeds or transfer them out of the country. Or he may give away all his valuable assets to his mistress to prevent his wife from getting her hands on them.

This chapter outlines the steps that can be taken to prevent a spouse from successfully escaping from his or her financial obligations after the divorce in this way. Whilst the chapter assumes that it is the husband who is attempting to shirk his responsibilities, the same principles apply if the wife attempts to defeat her husband's claims by making dispositions of her property.

1. The home: precautionary measures

In many cases, the family house will be not only your major asset but also the only place you have to live. It will therefore be vital to make sure that your husband cannot sell it without your consent.

If your name is on the title deeds of the property, there is no risk of your spouse disposing of it in any way without your knowledge. He will need your consent and your signature before he can mortgage the property or transfer it to anyone else by sale or gift.

Whilst it is likely that you would find out if your husband was trying to sell the house in which you are living, nevertheless, if the house is in your husband's sole name, he could theoretically conclude a deal without telling you anything about it because he will not need your consent or your signature to do so. To protect you against the risk of your husband dealing with the house in any way, against your will, your solicitor will probably consider registering a 'notice' or 'land charge'. Whenever a house is sold, a prospective purchaser makes various enquiries before he decides definitely that he will buy. As part of these enquiries, he will consult a register which shows whether anyone else has any rights in respect of the property. Your land charge or notice shows on this register that you have the right to occupy the property because you are married to the owner of it. A purchaser would be very unlikely to go ahead and buy the property once he found out about this. Even if he did, he would have to allow you to go on living there at least up to the date of the decree absolute of divorce and possibly even longer in some cases.

2. Seeking protection from the court: the home and other assets
If you can satisfy the court:

(i) that you have a claim to a share of the family assets or income

and (ii) that your spouse is about to make off with some of the assets to defeat your claim, or has already done so, the court may be able to step in and prevent the proposed dispositions taking place or set aside whatever transactions your spouse has already completed.

If you are seriously worried that your spouse is contemplating some sort of deal which will work to your disadvantage, contact your solictor *without delay*. There is far more that he can do to help you before the deal actually takes place than after it has been accomplished.

a) *Before the deal takes place*

The court can make an injunction to prevent your spouse from disposing of any of his or the family's assets, for example savings in a bank account, a valuable piece of furniture or the house itself. Disobedience to an injunction is punishable ultimately by imprisonment.

Alternatively the court can make an order that your spouse pay over money that he has to an independent person for safe keeping, for example into an account at the court or a bank account in the names of both your solicitors.

b) *After the deal has taken place*

You may not find out about your husband's activities until after he has put a large proportion of his assets out of your reach. Whether the court can then do anything to help you will depend on the circumstances in which your husband has disposed of the assets. The court has the power to set transactions aside, but only provided that they were not made with someone who paid a proper price and had no idea of your claim and your husband's intention to defeat it. Obviously it would be unfair if an honest person such as this, who had paid for the particular item, were to be deprived of it at a later stage. To give you an example, suppose that your husband puts all his stocks and shares into the name of his mother who pays him nothing for them and knows exactly what is going on – the court could set this transaction aside. Suppose however that your husband sells the stocks and shares to ordinary purchasers (who have no idea of the circumstances) and dissipates the proceeds – there is nothing the court can do to recover the stocks and shares for you.

20 Obtaining Financial Help Before Your Divorce Comes Through

As your marriage breaks down, you could find yourself facing pressing financial problems. If you have earnings or savings of your own, you may be able to cope, at least until a permanent financial agreement can be reached after the divorce. But some problems just will not wait. It is usually the wife who does not have independent resources and who suffers most acutely in the early stages if, for example, her husband stops paying her any housekeeping money or refuses to meet the household bills or to pay the mortgage. This chapter therefore assumes that it is the wife who will be seeking financial help; a husband would however be eligible to make an application to the court for maintenance from his wife or to claim state benefits in exactly the same way if he needed to do so.

Coping with your immediate problems

To begin with you will probably have to rely on whatever savings you have managed to accumulate and on borrowing whatever you can from relatives and friends. Whilst this may enable you to meet day to day living expenses, major bills such as the mortgage payments, the rates, gas and electricity are likely to remain a problem. Do not be afraid to approach the building society or authority concerned and explain your situation to them quite frankly -you will be surprised how sympathetic and accommodating they are in most cases.

Sooner or later, however, you will need assistance of a more positive kind. There are two ways in which you may be able to obtain financial help at this stage - by applying to the court for an order obliging your husband to maintain you and by applying for benefits of a social security nature such as supplementary benefit.

State and other benefits

There are various kinds of cash help available. You can obtain a copy of a very useful booklet known at the time of writing as 'Which Benefit?' from your local social security office. You will find the address of your local office listed in the telephone directory under 'Health and Social Security, Department of'. The booklet gives up to date information on the types of benefit currently available and you will be able to tell from it whether you are likely to be eligible for assistance. There is a variety of other books and leaflets available from a number of sources. For example, the Child Poverty Action group, based in London, publish several guides about benefits and also a regular bulletin.

The chart on the opposite page shows the benefits that are most likely to help you. None of them depends on whether you have made national insurance contributions. The chart assumes that you and your husband are living separately, even though you are not yet divorced. If you have not yet separated, you will

Type of benefit	*Do I qualify?*	*What form does the benefit take?*	*Further information about the benefit and how to apply*
1. Supplementary benefit	If you are not in full time work and your income is less than you need to live on, you may qualify. Your needs are assessed according to your circumstances (how many children you have living with you, what you pay for accommodation etc.). Do not expect the official estimate of your needs necessarily to coincide with what you think you require. If you have capital (over and above your house and personal possessions) that exceeds a fixed limit, you will not be entitled to benefit, whatever your income position.	Generally you receive a regular cash payment of the difference between your present income and your needs. Do not expect a great deal of money supplementary benefit does not provide for much more than the bare essentials. You are also automatically entitled to free dental treatment etc. (see under 3, below).	Leaflets are available from a social security office, post offices, Citizens' Advice Bureaux. If you need further help about your particular circumstances, you will be able to discuss your problems with someone at the social security office or a Citizens' Advice Bureau.
2. Family income supplement (FIS)	If you work full time (at least 24 hours a week for a parent living on her own) and you are looking after children, you may be eligible for FIS if your earnings fall below the level considered to be the minimum required by someone in your circumstances.	You receive a regular cash payment to bring your income up to the minimum level acceptable for someone with the number of children you have living with you. FIS is also your passport to other benefits such as dental treatment etc. (see under 3, below).	Leaflets are available from post offices, a social security office, Citizens' Advice Bureaux. You can claim this benefit by post claim forms come with the leaflets. Ask at a social security office or Citizens' Advice Bureau for personal advice.
3. Other benefits such as free milk, dental treatment, prescriptions	If you receive supplementary benefit or FIS, you are automatically entitled to these benefits. Even if you do not receive supplementary benefit or FIS, you may qualify for some of the benefits anyway for some other	You may be entitled to receive a range of services free of charge, for example, free milk for children under 5, free school meals, free dental treatment etc.	Leaflets are available from social security offices, post offices or Citizens' Advice Bureaux, and from other sources appropriate to the type of benefit you wish to claim, for example, if you want information

Type of benefit	*Do I qualify?*	*What form does the benefit take?*	*Further information about the benefit and how to apply*
	reason e.g. women who have had a baby in the past year are entitled to free dental treatment.		about benefits relating to your child at school, you should ask at your Education office. If you need personal advice on any point, ask first at the place where you collect the leaflet. If they cannot help you, they may be able to tell you who will.
4. Child benefit	If you are responsible for a child under 16, or under 19 and still studying at school or college up to and including A-levels, you should be eligible for child benefit. You can claim if the child is living with you or if you contribute towards his maintenance at a rate of at least the current child benefit rate. This could mean that both you and your husband would be eligible for the benefit. In these circumstances it is usual for the parent with whom the child is living to draw the benefit. If your husband is presently drawing the benefit and it has to be transferred to you, you can expect a delay before you get your order book which will entitle you to payments.	You can draw a regular fixed sum for each relevant child. If you are looking after a child on your own, you may be entitled to an additional sum each week by way of one parent benefit (see 5, below).	Leaflets are available from social security offices, post offices and Citizens' Advice Bureaux. Ask at the social security office or Citizens' Advice Bureau if you need personal advice.
5. One parent benefit	If you are looking after a child on your own because you are permanently separated from your husband, you may be eligible for one	You will receive a small additional benefit for one of your children, on top of your ordinary child benefit.	Leaflets are available from social security offices or Citizens' Advice Bureaux. Ask there for further information.

Type of benefit	*Do I qualify?*	*What form does the benefit take?*	*Further information about the benefit and how to apply*
	parent benefit. You will not be able to draw this extra benefit until you have been separated for 13 weeks, or until you are divorced or legally separated (by the court) if this comes through within the 13 weeks.		
6. Housing Benefit Rent allowances and rebates and rate rebates	If you have difficulty in paying your rent or rates, whether or not you are in work, you may be eligible for assistance. Whether you do receive help with your rent or rates will depend on your personal circumstances your income, whether you are on supplementary benefit, the amount of rent you pay, how many children you have living with you etc. Both private and council tenants are eligible for help with rent and even owner occupiers can get help with rates.	If you are a private tenant, you receive a rent allowance in cash. Council tenants receive help in the form of a reduction in the rent they have to pay. Rate rebates take the form of a reduction in the amount of rates you pay.	Leaflets are available from local council offices or Citizens' Advice Bureaux. Ask there about particular problems. Your claim will be made automatically for you if you are on supplementary benefit.

generally have great difficulty in obtaining benefits. This is because the benefit schemes are, on the whole, still geared to the sort of domestic arrangement where the husband is the breadwinner and provider for the family. Therefore most benefits are assessed according to his circumstances and paid to him.

If you are in financial difficulty whilst still living with your spouse, you should seek advice about state benefits from a Citizens' Advice Bureau or from your local Social Security office. You may, for example, be able to arrange for your husband's supplementary benefit to be paid to you instead of to him, if he is refusing to support you and the children properly. You should also be able to draw any child benefit to which your family is entitled yourself unless you have specifically assigned your right to do so to your husband.

Court orders

The help you can obtain through the courts depends on whether you or your spouse have yet started divorce proceedings. This chapter deals with the orders that can be made in your own favour. You should refer to Chapter 21 for details of the help that the courts can give once divorce proceedings are commenced in relation to any of the children that you have living with you. If you need financial help with the children before divorce proceedings are begun, the magistrates' court will usually have power to order maintenance for them and possibly also a lump sum payment.

1. If you or your spouse have already started divorce proceedings.

WHAT TYPE OF HELP CAN I GET?

The divorce court can order your husband to make regular cash payments to you to provide for your needs until the divorce comes through. Such payments are commonly referred to as 'maintenance'. Because the court's order is only temporary as yet, the official term for the maintenance ordered is 'maintenance pending suit' (in other words, maintenance while the divorce itself is being decided).

The court cannot order your husband to pay you a more substantial lump sum of money or deal with the ownership of your property (the house, furniture, car etc.) at this point; that will be sorted out after your divorce comes through. The court may, however, be able to make orders as to who is to live in the house if it is not possible for both of you to go on living there together (see Chapter 13). The court can also take steps to prevent either of you from disposing of any of your property before it has had the opportunity to consider what should be done with it in the future, if it feels that what you propose to do with the property will restrict its powers to achieve a fair long term arrangement for you both (see Chapter 19).

DOES IT MATTER WHO STARTED THE DIVORCE PROCEEDINGS?

It does not matter whether you or your husband started the divorce proceedings – either of you can apply for maintenance pending suit. It is no advantage to you when you apply for maintenance to be the one who started the divorce proceedings; your maintenance will not be increased if you are claiming a divorce or decreased if you are being divorced. Nor is the way you have both behaved relevant to the issues of finance or property unless one of you has behaved so badly that most right thinking people would consider it unfair that that spouse should receive a normal amount of maintenance or should still get his or her normal share in the family property.

WHEN DO I APPLY?

You can apply at any stage between the commencement of the divorce proceedings (when the divorce petition is filed with the court – see Chapter 8) and the date on which decree nisi of divorce is made absolute, whether or not you are living apart.

HOW LONG DOES AN ORDER FOR MAINTENANCE PENDING SUIT LAST?

Maintenance pending suit is only designed as a temporary measure to tide you over until your divorce is finalised and long term plans for your property and finances can be made and put into operation. Maintenance pending suit therefore ceases to be payable when your divorce is made absolute.

HOW MUCH MAINTENANCE WILL I GET?

It is not possible to tell you exactly how much maintenance pending suit you will get. A maintenance order is tailor made for you – it all depends on your personal income and requirements. Your application is considered by a Registrar who has to decide what maintenance would be reasonable in your case.

WHAT SORT OF CONSIDERATIONS ARE RELEVANT TO THE REGISTRAR'S DECISION?

The Registrar will look at the circumstances of both of you and concentrate on achieving a fair balance between what you need to provide a roof over your head and to look after your everyday needs and what your husband can afford to pay. You will both be expected to provide details of your income from all sources (earnings, child benefit, interest from savings accounts etc.) and your regular expenses (food, heating, rates, rent, mortgage, school dinners for the children, etc.). Assessing your income and expenses is not always completely straightforward; the following points quite often arise:

a) You may already be receiving social security benefits of a kind that depend on your means, for example supplementary benefit. These will not be counted as part of your steady income because as soon as you start to receive maintenance, your means go up and your social security benefits may therefore be reduced. Nevertheless, the Registrar can rely on the fact that, if your husband cannot afford to pay you anything at all, perhaps because he is unemployed, you will be provided for by the State.

b) You may have formed a relationship with another man. The mere fact that you may have committed adultery will not normally prevent you from getting maintenance from your husband. However, if you *live* with another man, he will probably help to provide for your everyday needs, for example you may live in his house instead of having to pay your own rent, electricity bills etc. or he may pay for food for the family or for your petrol or clothes. If you have this kind of relationship your need for maintenance from your husband will be reduced and you will find that you may no longer be eligible for maintenance or that the order you get will be very much reduced.

c) Resources available to you or your husband will not always take the form of money. Other resources can be taken into account such as board and lodging provided free with your job, luncheon vouchers, a company car.

If you want to get a rough idea of whether you would be entitled to any maintenance pending suit, you can draw up a balance sheet setting out your regular monthly or weekly income and your reasonable outgoings for the same period. If your income already equals or exceeds your expenses, you are unlikely to get maintenance pending suit although it is still worth asking your solicitor about it. If your income is less than your outgoings, you may well be eligible for maintenance pending suit provided that your husband is in a position to make payments to you (he may not be if, for example, he is unemployed). Your solicitor will have a look at all the figures and tell you whether you are likely to get an order. Because there is no mathematical formula for working out maintenance pending suit, he will not necessarily be able to tell you exactly what will be ordered, but he will be able to give you a good idea from his experience of cases such as yours.

You will find that some of the information provided in the following chapter on long term maintenance (periodical payments) is also relevant to your application for maintenance pending suit. However, you should bear in mind that whereas an order for periodical payments is made after a detailed consideration of all your circumstances and is usually meant to last for some considerable time, an order for maintenance pending suit is temporary and the Registrar may have to do the best he can to be fair on the limited information that is available so far about your circumstances. This may not include all the details he would like to know when he considers periodical payments. You can therefore often expect a maintenance pending suit order to be for rather less than a periodical payments order would be.

INTERIM MAINTENANCE PENDING SUIT

It sometimes happens that the Registrar is not in a position to make a maintenance pending suit order when he first considers your application. This can be for a variety of reasons, for example, he may not yet have sufficient information about your husband's financial position or he may feel that your case involves a complication that should be referred to a Judge to decide. Should this be the case, the Registrar can, if you need immediate help, make an even more temporary order called an 'interim maintenance pending suit order'. This is based on whatever evidence is available so far and lasts only until the court can consider your application for maintenance pending suit fully. You cannot expect an interim order to be more than rough and ready assistance to get you out of difficulties for the immediate future.

WHAT HAPPENS AT THE HEARING?

The hearing takes place in the Registrar's private room. Both you and your husband will be required to swear affidavits setting out details of your financial position for the Registrar. The hearing will be relatively informal. You will both be expected to attend and either of you can be required to answer questions for the court about your circumstances. The hearing will not normally last very long. The Registrar will announce his decision there and then. He will tell you how much maintenance he is ordering and when the order will come into effect. If you are receiving social security benefits, you may well find that the order does not come into effect for fourteen days. This is to give the court time to notify the social security authorities of the order so that they can adjust your benefit to take account of the maintenance you will be receiving. The court can, if it thinks fit, backdate its order so that it is taken to have commenced before the date on which the order was actually made, provided that the starting date is not earlier than the date when the divorce petition was first presented. This is not done automatically because it means that if your husband has not been paying maintenance for you already at or over the rate ordered, he will be faced at the very beginning with the hardship of a bill for the arrears of maintenance that arise from the backdating of the order. If he has been paying already, he can be given credit for the payments that he has made and it may actually be to his advantage from a tax point of view to have the order backdated as it may mean that he can get tax relief for the payments that he would not otherwise have been able to claim (see Chapter 22). On the other hand, it may involve you in a tax liability because the maintenance you received becomes part of your income whereas if you had received it on a voluntary basis and not as part of a court order, you would not have had to pay tax on it. The Registrar will weigh up all the pros and cons of backdating the maintenance order and make the appropriate order for your case.

2. If neither of you has yet commenced divorce proceedings

If neither of you has yet started divorce proceedings, you will not be able to apply to the Divorce Court for maintenance pending suit. Nevertheless, there are other ways in which you can obtain assistance from the courts; the Magistrates' Court can be particularly helpful in these circumstances. Although orders for maintenance for children are not mentioned here, it should usually be possible to obtain a Magistrates' Court maintenance order in relation to a child who is living with you.

WHAT ORDERS CAN THE MAGISTRATES' COURT MAKE ABOUT FINANCE?

In order to obtain help with your financial situation from a Magistrates' Court, you must be able to show that you are eligible for a Magistrates' Court order. The chart below sets out the ways in which you can qualify for an order and the type of order that can be made.

If you can prove that:-	*You can obtain an order for:-*
i) your husband has deserted you ii) your husband has behaved unreasonably iii) your husband has failed to provide reasonable maintenance for you iv) your husband has failed to provide or make reasonable contribution towards the maintenance of a child of the family	maintenance for yourself (payable weekly or at any other interval) and/or a lump sum payment of not more than £500.
v) you and your husband have come to a financial arrangement that you would both like the court to put into an order.	maintenance for yourself in the form you have agreed and/or a lump sum payment of the amount you have agreed upon (which can exceed £500).
vi) you and your husband have been separated by agreement for more than 3 months and your husband has in fact been making maintenance payments to you and you would like to have the security of an order.	maintenance (but not a lump sum) for yourself of an amount that must not exceed, over any 3 month period, the total of payments you have received over the 3 months immediately before you made your application.

HOW DO THE MAGISTRATES DECIDE ON THE AMOUNT OF THE ORDER?

The magistrates will fix the amount of maintenance they order in much the same way as the divorce court decides on the amount of periodical payments you should receive after your divorce (see Chapter 21). The amount of any lump sum will depend on what you need, what expenses you incurred in maintaining yourself or a child of the family before you made your application to the court, and how much your husband can afford to pay.

WHAT IF WE ARE STILL LIVING TOGETHER?

If you are living together when you make your application to the magistrates' court, you can still obtain an order from the court (although not, of course, on the basis of separation for 3 months, see vi) above). However, if you go on living together for a continuous period of more than 6 months after the order is made, an order for maintenance will cease to be effective.

If you are living apart when you get an order but you subsequently start to live together again, your maintenance order will cease if you live together for a continous period of more than 6 months. An order made under (vi) above will cease at once if you start to live together again.

If you require maintenance at any stage after your maintenance order has ceased, you will have to apply to the court again.

3. The relationship between maintenance pending suit and magistrates' orders

WHAT IF WE ARE THINKING OF GETTING DIVORCED – IS IT WORTH APPLYING FOR A MAGISTRATES' COURT ORDER?

It really depends on your particular circumstances. If you are about to start divorce proceedings, you will probably be wasting your time applying to the magistrates' court – it would be better to get on with starting the divorce proceedings and apply for maintenance pending suit from the divorce court. If you really are not sure what to do about a divorce and some time is likely to elapse before you are ready to start divorce proceedings, you may need to apply to the magistrates' court meanwhile. Your solicitor will advise you as to the best course to take.

DO I NEED TO INVOLVE THE DIVORCE COURT IN MY FINANCES IF I ALREADY HAVE A MAGISTRATES' COURT ORDER FOR MAINTENANCE WHEN I OR MY HUSBAND START DIVORCE PROCEEDINGS?

Whether you need to do anything further to tide you over until after the divorce, will depend on your circumstances. If you are satisfied with the magistrates' order, you can rely on that until the divorce court sorts out your property and finance after the divorce. If you require more than you are getting under the magistrates' court order, your solicitor will advise you as to whether you should return to the magistrates' court to have your order put up or apply to the divorce court for maintenance pending suit.

Once your divorce comes through you will normally want the divorce court to sort out your long-term arrangements over property and finance for you. Therefore, whilst your magistrates' court order will not automatically end when you are divorced, it is usually convenient for the divorce court to terminate the magistrates' court order and reconsider the whole question of your finances and property itself at that stage.

If the magistrates' court order should continue after your divorce, maintenance will nevertheless cease to be payable if you, the recipient, then remarry.

An order for a lump sum payment made by the magistrates is normally a 'once and for all' order and is not affected by anything that occurs after it has been paid, be it living together, a divorce or your remarrying.

WHY BOTHER TO APPLY FOR A COURT ORDER IF I CAN DRAW STATE BENEFITS?

Many people are reluctant to rely on state benefits of any kind and are therefore anxious to obtain a maintenance order against their husband so that they no longer need to do so. Even if you do not feel like this, you are quite likely to be better off if you are receiving maintenance, provided that your husband is in a position to pay more than the current rates of benefit in maintenance. You may also find that the social security authorities suggest to you that you go to court to obtain an order against your husband because this will relieve them of at least some of their liability towards you. It is up to you whether you comply with their wishes. If you do not and you are still married, they will probably be able to take the matter into their own hands and apply to court for an order against your husband themselves.

21
Long Term Arrangements over Property and Finance

What to do about the house, how to share out your other property and how to make sure that you both have sufficient income for the future will no doubt be questions that have been preying on your mind since you first realised that your marriage was at an end. You may have tackled the problems on a temporary basis even before your divorce was granted. Once the divorce itself is out of the way, you will have to take the bull by the horns and come to a permanent arrangement.

If you and your spouse are able to come to an agreement about some or all of these questions, so much the better. You should find Chapter 18 helpful in pointing out some of the practical matters that you need to consider in relation to your agreement. As you will see it is often prudent to have your agreement made formal by means of a court order so that there can be no disagreement in the future about its terms and so that you can be sure that you are both bound by it.

Read Chapter 22 in conjunction with this chapter – it deals with the tax implications of court orders and agreements and will enable you to make sure that you will not be paying more tax than is necessary as a result of your financial arrangements.

If you cannot agree as to what should happen, you can ask the court to decide for you. It is normally the job of a Registrar of the divorce court to consider your case and formulate your future arrangements for you. His final order will be tailor-made for you. There is no universal formula that you can use to work out what will be decided in your case. However, this chapter will give you a guide as to the sort of solution the court might impose for your problems. If you feel that you would like more personal advice, your solicitor should be able to make an assessment of the likely outcome of the case for you. However, even he can never be certain what the court will decide because the scope of potential court orders is so wide.

NOTE
You can appeal against what you think is a wrongful court order but you may have to be quick – see page 180

How to use this chapter
This chapter is divided into 4 parts.
Part I outlines the wide range of orders that the Registrar can make when he considers your case.
Part II describes the considerations that the Registrar will take into account and indicates how he might approach particular problems that arise.
Part III gives a number of examples of actual cases in which the court has reached a solution of the various problems facing the

families concerned on divorce.

Part IV deals with the actual court hearing – who has to arrange it, how soon can it take place, what happens etc.

Financial arrangements for the children are, for the most part, dealt with separately in this chapter to avoid confusion. In fact, in the majority of cases, the Registrar will consider all the arrangements for the family as a whole (parents and children) at the same time since they are so interdependent.

PART 1. THE ORDERS THAT THE COURT CAN MAKE

The court has far reaching powers to adjust your rights to property and income after the divorce to make sure that proper provision is made for the whole family. The range of potential orders comprises two categories:

(1) orders concerned with income (often referred to as 'financial provision orders');

(2) orders concerned with the family's capital assets (often referred to as 'property adjustment orders').

(1) Financial provision orders

FOR HUSBAND AND WIFE: there are three types of financial provision order that the court can make:–

(a) an order for periodical payments. This is commonly known as a 'maintenance order'. It obliges one spouse to pay the other a sum of money at regular intervals, usually every week or every month. The payment is normally designed to go towards living expenses. An order for periodical payments will end automatically on the death or remarriage of the recipient or on the death of the payer.

(b) an order for secured periodical payments. This is an order for maintenance coupled with an order that the payer of the maintenance should guarantee the payments in some way, for example by setting aside assets, such as shares, that will produce sufficient income to cover the maintenance ordered. It will end automatically if the recipient dies or remarries, but it will not necessarily end on the death of the payer. The courts do not often make orders for secured periodical payments unless the family concerned is fairly wealthy.

(c) a lump sum order. This is an order whereby one spouse is ordered to pay the other a rather more substantial sum of money. It is different from the payment of maintenance because it is generally a 'once-and-for-all' payment (although it can sometimes be handed over in instalments), whereas maintenance imposes a continuing obligation to pay at regular intervals over a period of time.

FOR THE CHILDREN: subject to certain age limits, the court is able to make the same financial provision orders in favour of a child of the family as it can make in favour of either spouse. So it can order one of you to pay maintenance or secured maintenance for a child within the following age limits:

- in the first place, the order must not extend beyond the child's 17th birthday
- however, the court can specifically order that it should continue until the child is 18
- and if the child is or will be receiving instruction at an educational establishment or undergoing training for a trade, profession or vocation (whether or not he is also earning) or there are special circumstances that justify the making of an order regardless of the child's age (for instance if he is physically or mentally handicapped), the court can order payments beyond the child's 18th birthday.

Lump sum orders can also be made in favour of children who are within the relevant age limits, but are, in fact, fairly seldom made unless the child's family is relatively wealthy, or the child has a special need for capital.

(2) Property adjustment orders

FOR HUSBAND AND WIFE: the court's powers are so far-reaching in relation to property that, basically, it can reallocate all your property (house, furniture, shares etc. etc.) between you in whatever way it sees fit. For example, it can order one of you to transfer property that you own to the other or to share it with your spouse or to settle it on trust for your spouse or to sell it and divide the proceeds between you and so on.

FOR THE CHILDREN: the court can even allocate some of your property to your children if this seems appropriate. However, most families cannot afford to benefit the children directly in this way as they need all their assets to provide for themselves and the children (for a home, furnishings, etc.) after the divorce. The court will therefore only contemplate transferring some of your assets to your children if you are very well off.

The court can, of course, combine several orders in one case. It is common therefore to find that the court makes an order in relation to the matrimonial home *and* orders one spouse to pay maintenance to the other spouse and the children.

PART II. THE COURT'S APPROACH TO THE PROBLEM

1. Taking stock

The court will need to know exactly what assets and earning power you have between you and what you are both going to need for the future by way of capital and income.

You may find it helpful (for your own purposes as well as for the court) to draw up a balance sheet listing your joint assets and requirements in two columns; 'Assets' and 'Needs'. In your assets column, you will have to list two kinds of asset – *capital* assets such as your house (whether you own or rent it), car, furniture, savings, insurance policies, business interests etc. and *income* which will probably be mainly from your employment but may also be derived from investments etc. Try to put a value on your capital assets. A rough guide may be sufficient with assets such as the contents of the house but the court will require a more exact estimate with more valuable items such as the house itself. Your solicitor will normally be able to arrange for a formal valuation of the house by an estate agent if necessary (or you can) and he may well be able to agree with your spouse or his or her solicitor that you will both abide by the valuation of one estate agent and share his charges rather than going to the expense of obtaining two separate valuations. You will need to know how much is outstanding on any loan or mortgage that you took in order to purchase the house – details of this can be obtained from your bank or building society. You will also have to bear in mind that if you intend to sell the house, you will have to meet legal and estate agent's fees in respect of the sale. Consider whether each of your assets could be easily realised if necessary – some may not be realisable, for example, you may have the use of a company car but obviously would not be able to transfer the car to your spouse or sell it even if you wanted to, or you may have business assets that you could not sell without damaging your business.

In your needs column, it is likely that the major requirements of both of you will be a home (together with furnishings and furniture) and sufficient income after tax on which to live.

2. Finding a starting point for the court's order

If you asked the court to determine a dispute between you and your neighbour as to, say, who was entitled to use a particular strip of land on your joint boundary, the court would decide the question simply by examining the evidence to see which of you actually owned the land. Considerations of whether it was *fair* that the person owned the land and who *needed* it most would not enter into the decision.

When you ask the court to determine what should happen to your family assets and income after your divorce however, the court has a free hand to do whatever is fair and practical. Instead of being the *only* consideration, the question of ownership becomes merely one of the many factors that the court can take into account in reaching its decision, and not a very important factor at that. This means that, for example, even if the family home is in the husband's name alone, the wife may well be entitled to a share in its value on divorce – indeed, if necessary, the court can order that it should be transferred into her name entirely. The same is true of all the family's assets.

With such a wide scope, how does the Registrar know where to start? There is really nothing precise and scientific about his decision at all – if you asked him how he arrived at a particular solution he would probably say it was what he *felt* was right, using his experience and a bit of trial, error and imagination. However the law does require him to take into account all the circumstances of the case and his attention is particularly directed to certain matters which are dealt with in the following sections of this part of the Chapter.

You may also hear people talk about something called 'the one third rule' in connection with the financial side of divorce. In the recent past this 'rule' has been widely used by Registrars as a starting point for their consideration of particular cases and is the nearest there has been to a mathematical formula for deciding what should happen. It envisages that, in a typical dispute between husband and wife over property and maintenance, the fair solution may well be for the wife to have one third of the family's capital assets and to have whatever income she is able to earn herself made up to the equivalent of one third of her and her husband's joint incomes by way of maintenance payments from him in the future. The typical case on which this rule is based is where a couple marry with very little in the way of capital and over a number of years of marriage, acquire their own home (or a fairly substantial equity in it, even if some money is outstanding on mortgage) and possibly build up some savings. In this typical family, the money to do this is provided largely by the husband, because the wife has been at home looking after him and the children for a substantial part of the marriage. It is contemplated that she will continue to be dependent on the husband for maintenance.

However nowadays many wives continue to work throughout much of their marriage and contribute significantly to family finances. Furthermore, both the courts and couples themselves are tending to prefer a clean break after divorce if possible with the wife no longer dependent on the husband for maintenance. This means that, although Registrars will probably continue to bear the one third rule in mind, it is likely to have less and less influence on their decisions and will not, therefore, help you to forecast the possible outcome of your case.

Having worked out roughly the result that the one third rule would produce in a particular case, the court has then to make allowances for the special circumstances of the family concerned.

The following sections of this part of the chapter show exactly what circumstances are relevant and how they might affect the court's ultimate decision.

3. The considerations that the court has to bear in mind

The law provides that in deciding on the orders it should make, the court should give first consideration to the welfare during their childhood of any children of the family who are under 18 but must also take into account all the circumstances of the case. In the case of provision for a husband or wife, these circumstances include:–

a) the income, earning capacity, property and other financial resources which each of you has or is likely to have in the foreseeable future;

b) the financial needs, obligations and responsibilities that each of you has or is likely to have in the foreseeable future;

c) the standard of living that you enjoyed as a family before the breakdown of your marriage;

d) how old you both are and how long the marriage has lasted;

e) any physical or mental disabilities that either of you have;

f) the contributions that you have both made or are likely to make in the foreseeable future to the welfare of the family (not only financial contributions but also, for example, contributions by looking after the home and caring for the family);

g) whether either of you will lose the chance of acquiring any benefit (for example a widow's pension) as a result of the divorce;

h) in some cases, the conduct of each of you.

Remarriage is not one of the circumstances that the court is specifically directed to take into account. Nevertheless, it can be relevant to the court's decision and you should see Chapter 25 for a summary of the effects of remarriage and the prospect of remarriage on orders of the court in relation to property and finance.

When considering what provision to make for your children, the court is directed to consider very similar factors, for example what the child needs, what resources he has (if any), whether he has any disabilities etc. It can also consider how you and your spouse had intended the child to be educated and trained, so if, for instance, you had originally intended the child to go to a fee paying school, the court will try to come to an arrangement that will enable the parent with custody to go ahead with the plan.

Some of these factors need further explanation:

INCOME AND EARNING CAPACITY:

(i) *What is a man's income?* The court will look at the income of each of you before tax, taking into account the expenses that you incur to earn it (for example National Insurance contributions, travelling expenses etc.). If you are employed, your income will be apparent from your past pay slips. If you are self-employed, the court will have a look at your past years' accounts. If you receive state benefits that are not means-tested, these will be taken into account (for example, child benefit). On the other hand, benefits that depend on your means, such as supplementary benefit, will generally be ignored because they will be affected by whatever order the court makes.

(ii) *Perks.* Many employees nowadays receive perks from their employers, for instance the use of a company car, luncheon vouchers, a regular Christmas bonus etc. Self-employed people often derive similar advantages in kind through their businesses. The court can take this kind of advantage into account.

(iii) *The unemployed husband.* If a man is unemployed through no fault of his own, the court will not make an order that he would only be able to afford to pay from regular earnings. On the other hand, if he is voluntarily out of work and there is employment available for him if he chose to take it, the court might decide to put pressure on him to go back to work by, say, making a maintenance order that he could only afford to pay if he was earning a regular wage.

(iv) *Can a wife be made to work?* It is within the court's power to decide that a wife should receive reduced or no maintenance or to grant her maintenance for a limited period only because she should be working. However, it will never do this unless it is clear that there are jobs available that she could do.

If employment is available for the wife, the court will not penalise her for not taking it until it has gone into all the circumstances. It will look at your past arrangements about work. If, with the husband's agreement, the wife has never worked during the marriage, the court will not necessarily ask her to go out and get a job just because she has got divorced. On the other hand, if she has got a job, she will not be able to give it up and rely on her husband to support her after the divorce. Furthermore, if she is young with no children and can get a job, she will generally be expected to do so to relieve her husband of responsibility for her – the courts encourage arrangements that can achieve a completely clean break between husband and wife.

If there are children who need looking after, this will obviously affect the wife's ability to work. It is generally accepted that the wife is entitled to stay at home to look after young children (even if they have reached school age) unless of course, she has previously been accustomed to working *and* bringing up the family during the marriage. This may mean that she cannot work at all, or that she can only be expected to do a part time job.

(v) *The resources of a new partner.* If either of you remarries or starts to live with a new partner, this will obviously affect your financial position for better or worse. The court will not give your former spouse a share in the income or assets of your new partner. However, if your new partner pools his or her resources with you, you may find that you have more income and assets available to maintain your former spouse and children. This will be taken into account.

NEEDS AND OBLIGATIONS ETC.:

(i) *A home.* Both of you will probably need a home for yourself (and the children). The court will concentrate very much on making sure that everyone has a roof over their head for the future.

(ii) *Mortgages and loans.* In making arrangements for your future, you may well run into debt. If you have had to borrow money for reasonable purposes, for instance to buy yourself somewhere to live, the court will take account of the fact that you will have to repay this sum with interest.

(iii) *Obligations to a new partner.* Far from providing you with additional resources, your new partner may be a drain on your income. You may need to provide him or her with a home, housekeeping etc. The court will take this into account in assessing your position but will look upon your obligations to your former family as equally important.

(iv) *Ensuring you both have enough income for your needs.* Where a couple have a very low income between them, the court will have to concentrate particularly on providing for their essential needs. The court will make sure that, if it orders one spouse to maintain the other, this will not reduce that spouse's income for his own needs below subsistence level. If this means that he cannot be ordered to pay the other spouse sufficient for her needs, she will have to rely on state benefits to make up the shortfall.

HOW LONG THE MARRIAGE HAS LASTED: Obviously a wife with no children to look after who has been married for only a short time has less right to call on her husband for continuing maintenance and a share in his capital assets than a wife who has been married for some years and has brought up or is bringing up children. A young wife with no children after a short marriage can often only expect to get out of the marriage the equivalent of what she put into it. In other words, she will be entitled to a share in the capital assets only if she contributed to them financially or by her own efforts (for example by helping with building work involved in improving a house) and will be unlikely to receive maintenance.

YOUR CONTRIBUTIONS TO THE WELFARE OF THE FAMILY: Many couples make equal contributions to family life, although in different ways. Often the wife makes her contribution by caring for the family and the husband makes his by working and contributing financially. In some cases however, one spouse makes a greater contribution than the other, for example because he or she had substantial assets before the marriage or because he or she inherits from a relative during the marriage. In such a situation, it may well be fair for that spouse to take a larger share of the family assets when the marriage breaks down.

THE CONDUCT OF BOTH OF YOU: When a marriage breaks down, a fair share of the blame usually attaches to both parties. So in most cases, the way in which you have both behaved will not affect the court's decision on your property or maintenance. However, there are two situations in which conduct can affect the court's order:

(i) if either of you has behaved so badly that most ordinary people would feel that he or she should not receive as much income or property as usual, the court can adjust its order appropriately. For example, in one case, the court ordered a husband to transfer all his interest in the house to his wife because he had savaged her with a knife causing her serious injuries. Adultery plain and simple will not normally affect the order. However, it may do so if it occurs in particularly unpleasant circumstances (and possibly if it actually brings about the end of the marriage). So, for example, the court has, in the past, taken into account that a husband had committed adultery with his daughter-in-law.

(ii) if you start to live with someone else who supports you, this will be taken into account in assessing what orders should be made in your favour. And, of course, if you actually remarry, you will automatically lose your right to maintenance for yourself.

4. Coping with particular problems

a) THE HOUSE

(i) *If one or both of you own the house (whether or not subject to a mortgage):*

As made clear by the examples in Part III of this chapter, when it comes to dealing with the matrimonial home, the court will attempt to arrive at an arrangement that ensures that both of you and particularly the children have a home, whilst still rewarding you both fairly for the contributions that you have made to the marriage generally and to the acquisition of the house and other assets in particular.

This is not always possible. One spouse (usually the one with custody of the children) may therefore come away from the marriage with more capital than seems strictly fair in relation to his or her contribution because this is the only way to ensure that he or she is able to get somewhere to live after the divorce.

Generally, if you are accustomed to owning your own house or to be buying it on a mortgage, the court will try to devise an arrangement for the future that will enable both of you to continue as an owner/occupier. However, this cannot always be done and as a last resort, the court may have to come down in favour of an arrangement that provides one of you (normally the spouse looking after the children) with a home of your own and obliges the other to rely on rented accommodation, at least for the time being.

The court usually has a number of options in relation to the house. Basically there are two main sorts of arrangement possible – those that involve a sale of the house and those that enable one of you to continue to live in the house. The following are the more common alternatives open to the court, although others will no doubt present themselves in individual cases:–

– the court can order that the house should be *sold* at once and the proceeds divided between you as it thinks fair. This is really only practical when the proceeds of sale will be sufficiently large to enable both of you to obtain alternative accommodation. If either of you will be able to obtain a mortgage to assist in such a purchase, the court can take this into account. However this will not always be possible, particularly for a wife who is entirely dependent on maintenance. The court may therefore have to consider giving a larger share to the spouse who cannot obtain a mortgage so that he or she can buy a place outright, whilst the other spouse receives sufficient to make a deposit on a property to buy with a mortgage. The one thing the court will not want to do is to order a sale of your house which will give you both some capital but to neither of you enough to buy another property – with the result that you will both have to find rented accommodation (see Case 4 page 151).

– the court can order that the house should be *sold but postpone the sale* to some time in the future. This used to be done quite frequently where one spouse was looking after the children and needed to go on living in the house to provide them with a home. The court used to postpone the sale until the youngest child reached 17 or 18. Nowadays this type of order is not generally favoured by the courts because it is artificial to look on family life as ending when the children reach 17 or 18 – many children live with their parents, at least in holidays from college or university, for some time after their 17th or 18th birthdays. However, it may still be the only solution in some cases (see Cases 2 and 3 on page 150).

– the court can order that the house be allocated to one of you but give the other the *right to part of the proceeds of sale when the house is eventually sold.* This normally means that one of you has all the rights of an owner over the house and can decide when and if to sell it, but the other is deprived of both his home and capital asset at least for the time being. Before it makes an order of this kind therefore, the court will want to make sure that whoever does not have the house can get somewhere else to live. Sometimes this presents no real problem because he has already found a new home (perhaps because he has remarried and moved in to live with a new partner, or because he has the benefit of accommodation that comes with a job, or because he has already made arrangements to buy another property). In other cases, the court will try to make the arrangement fair by giving the spouse who does not get the home the lion's share of the family's other assets which he can use to make a deposit on a new house (see Case 6 on page 153).

– the court can allocate the house to one of you and order that spouse to pay the other a *lump sum* forthwith in compensation. Whether this is feasible will depend on how much the spouse with the house can raise (a loan or mortgage may present insuperable problems for a spouse dependent on maintenance) and how much, if anything, the other spouse needs to purchase alternative accommodation (see Case 1 on page 149).

– the court can allocate the house to one spouse and *compensate* the other spouse by, for example, relieving him or her of the obligation to pay any maintenance for the spouse who receives the house (see Case 5 on page 152).

(ii) *Rented homes:*
If you rent your home from the council or from a private landlord, the court can generally allocate the tenancy to one of you, irrespective of whose name it is in. It would be most likely to do this in favour of the spouse who has custody of the children.

b) THE CONTENTS OF THE HOUSE AND OTHER ASSETS
You will find the court reluctant to get involved in disputes between you over routine items of furniture and furnishings. You will be expected to decide between you what should happen to each item. People often find it convenient for the spouse who is to go on living in the matrimonial home to take the contents of the house, whilst the other spouse can be compensated by receiving other assets such as the car or a caravan. Each spouse will normally be entitled to his or her personal belongings, for instance clothes, jewellery etc. and to things given to him or her personally.

If you fail to agree and you ask the court to sort things out for you, you may well find that it simply orders that the whole lot be sold and the proceeds divided between you. You will both be the losers in this event as the property will inevitably fetch far less than it is worth to you or than it would cost to replace it.

c) VALUABLE ASSETS SUCH AS SAVINGS, ANTIQUES, STOCKS AND SHARES

What becomes of assets such as these will often depend on the arrangement made in relation to the house. They may be required to even out the distribution of capital between you. If not, the court will divide them in whatever way seems fair bearing in mind your needs and the way in which the assets were originally acquired. For example, a valuable antique inherited from the husband's family might be allocated to the husband and an oil painting owned by the wife before the marriage to her, whilst savings accumulated by them jointly during the marriage might be shared equally between them.

d) BUSINESSES

If one of you owns a business that is, strictly speaking, property that the court can reallocate between you on divorce. In practice, the court is unlikely to make any order that will damage your business interests or force you to sell up. Nor will you be required to take your spouse into partnership with you.

However, if your spouse has helped you to build up your business (for example by serving in your shop, or by doing the books, or helping in your hotel, or simply by staying at home and looking after domestic arrangements so that you are free to get on with your work) he or she will be entitled to have the value of this help reflected in the share he or she gets in the other family assets.

e) MAINTENANCE

(i) *For husband or wife:*

Both husbands and wives are entitled to apply for maintenance. However, by far the majority of claims are made by wives and this section therefore deals with a wife's claim to maintenance. The same principles apply to a husband's claim.

The trend recently has been towards enabling a couple to achieve a clean break from each other whenever possible after divorce. If maintenance has to be paid from one to the other, a clean break will not be possible. The court is therefore likely to investigate the possibility of an arragement that does not involve maintenance such as giving the wife a rather larger than average share of the family's capital assets so that she can be self-supporting.

Many couples are not however in a position to make a clean break. If the court has to make a maintenance order, it may fix the amount simply by careful consideration of your particular circumstances or it may use the 'one third rule' (see page 138) as a starting point. Using the 'one third rule' means calculating the sum of your joint incomes before deduction of tax but after deducting certain expenses, particularly the expenses that you both incur earning your income. Let us assume that you earn £90 a week (before deduction of tax but after you have paid your expenses) and your husband earns £270 per week. This gives a joint income of £360 per week. The court then divides this figure by 3, giving £120 per week. It then works out how much maintenance you would need from your husband to make your income up to this one third figure. In this example, you would need £120 - £90 = £30. If you earn the equivalent of one third of your joint income or more already, you would require no maintenance from your husband on this formula.

– the court then looks at the impact of tax on each of your incomes assuming that it makes an order in accordance with the one third rule and taking into account any order it is going to make in relation to the children. (See Chapter 22 for tax implications).

– the court can then calculate how much money you will each have in your pockets with which to meet your living expenses, from mortgage repayments and school fees to food and clothes. If necessary it will have to adjust the figure it had originally arrived at to make sure that you both have enough for your reasonable needs. It will check that your husband will not be reduced below subsistence level by the maintenance order, and, if the worst comes to the worst, it will have to reduce the amount of maintenance he is liable to pay and leave you to rely on state benefits (such as supplementary benefit) to bring you up to a satisfactory (in the eyes of our welfare system) standard of living.

– the court will then check that the order it has arrived at will fit in with all the circumstances of *your particular* case – for example, if you are already receiving a larger than average share of the capital assets, it might reduce your maintenance order to take account of this, or if you have been married for only a short time, it might decide to award you rather less than normal maintenance.

Once the correct order has been arrived at, the court must

consider when it should commence. It can backdate the order if it thinks fit but will consider the factors mentioned on page 129 under 'What happens at the hearing?' before doing so.

If you already have an order for maintenance pending suit that you obtained earlier in the divorce proceedings and you are content with the amount of maintenance you are receiving under it, you can simply ask the court to make an order in the same terms after the divorce. There is no need to have the whole matter reconsidered by the court, unless your spouse insists upon it.

Similarly if you can manage to agree on the amount of the maintenance order, you can ask the court merely to make an order in the terms you have agreed.

A maintenance order is not final – it can be varied at a later date if circumstances warrange a change (see Chapter 24).

Normally you will receive your maintenance direct from your husband. However the court can direct that the maintenance order should be registered in a magistrates' court (see Chapter 23). If this is done, your husband will pay the maintenance to the magistrates' court who will forward it to you. If you have any problems in obtaining your maintenance, you should refer to Chapter 23 which deals with the enforcement of orders.

(ii) *For the children:*
The court has a free hand to make whatever orders for maintenance for the children seem right. Probably the most important deciding factor is what the children need. In suitable cases, maintenance for a child can even include sufficient money to cover his school fees.

The court can order either of you to maintain a child of which you are not actually a parent if that child has been treated by both of you as a child of your family (see page 52 – for example, a husband can be ordered to maintain a child of the wife by a former marriage). However, when making a maintenance order for a child in these circumstances, the court will investigate whether any other person has a duty to maintain that child (in the example just given, the wife's former spouse could have such a duty). It will also take into account how much you have contributed to the child's maintenance in the past and whether you made these contributions knowing that the child was not actually your own. On the whole therefore, you are likely to have to pay less maintenance for a child of which you are not the parent (unless, of course, you have adopted the child) than you are for your own child.

The court can order you to pay maintenance direct to the child (which often has tax advantages – see Chapter 22), or to your spouse for the child's benefit, or even to the child's school for his benefit if the maintenance concerned is to cover school fees. If you are ordered to pay money to your child's school you should pay the appropriate amount to the person named in the court order. This may be the headmaster, bursar or other responsible person. If you are ordered to pay maintenance to the child or to your spouse for the benefit of the child, you can usually hand over the money direct to your spouse rather than giving it to the child himself.

PART III. EXAMPLES FROM DECIDED CASES

The cases described in this section actually happened. None of the situations are particularly out of the ordinary and you may find that some are very similar to your own. However, decisions made for other families can never be any more than a guide as to the likely outcome of your own case and, even if the situation described seems almost identical, do not assume that the outcome will necessarily be the same for you.

The cases are largely about the family home – this being one of the main sources of disagreement after a divorce. Many families also have difficulty in agreeing how much, if any, maintenance one spouse should pay to the other or to the children. However, you will notice that the question of maintenance does not feature very frequently in the examples given. This is because, as the previous part of this chapter shows, an assessment of the appropriate maintenance for a family will involve a detailed consideration of that family's income and outgoings. It would not therefore be very helpful to reproduce those details here, particularly as they are unlikely to be the same for another family and also because the effects of inflation soon cause the court's decision to be outdated and even misleading.

Case 1

A husband and wife had been married for nearly twenty years. He was a dentist. They had two children. The wife left home and they were divorced. The son, who was aged 13, lived with his father in the family home in the school holidays and attended a boarding school during term time where his fees were paid by his grandfather. The daughter, aged 11, lived with her mother. The family home had been bought shortly after the marriage. It was in the husband's name and was worth (free of mortgage) approximately £20,000 when the case came to be decided in 1973. The husband was earning at least £6,000 per annum before tax and the wife could earn £750 per annum before tax by part time work. The husband did not have any ready capital.

The court decided that the husband should be allocated the family home. However, the wife had made a substantial contribution to the family as a wife and mother and she deserved some compensation for losing the right to benefit from the home. It was therefore ordered that the husband should pay her a lump sum of £6,000 (nearly a third of the value of the house). It was felt this should be enough to enable her to put down a substantial deposit on a new home. The court decided that the husband should also pay her part of his income each year by way of maintenance (from which she should, with her own earnings, be able to meet mortgage repayments on her new home as well as providing for her living expenses). The figure fixed by the court was £1,500 per annum. When added to the £750 that the wife could be expected to earn herself, this would mean that she would be in receipt of roughly one third of their joint incomes. The husband was also ordered to pay £300 per annum by way of maintenance for the daughter.

Case 2

A husband and wife had been married for 15 years when the husband left home to live with another woman. They had no children and the wife stayed on in the matrimonial home, on her own. She obtained a divorce and asked the court to determine what was to happen to the home which was in the husband's name. Neither the husband nor the wife had any other capital assets of value. The husband was living with another woman in her council house and intended to marry her. He was going to arrange for the council tenancy to be transferred into the joint names of himself and his new partner. He was 43 and was earning slightly more than the wife who was 46.

The court was most concerned that the wife should have somewhere to live. The husband had secure accommodation already and did not need any money immediately to buy accommodation for himself. The court therefore decided that the wife should be allowed to go on living in the house for as long as she wanted or until she remarried. When she died, or moved, or remarried, she and the husband would be entitled to half the value of the house each.

(There is no magic in the fact that it was the wife who needed a home in this case. In another case, the court permitted a husband to stay in the house where he was looking after the children. The wife had remarried to a doctor and was not in need of accommodation. When the house was eventually sold on the husband's death, the proceeds were to be shared evenly between his estate and the wife.)

Case 3

The husband and wife were married for approximately 15 years and had one child of nearly 9 years old. By the time the court came to determine the question of their property and finance, they both intended to marry again and the income of the new families was going to very similar. The matrimonial home was in the joint names of the husband and wife, and the wife and child were still living there, whereas the husband was living with the lady he intended to marry.

The court decided that the wife and child should be allowed to go on living in the house until the child was 17. The wife was to be responsible for all the outgoings in relation to the house and the mortgage interest (though not the capital repayments on the mortgage which would be the joint responsibility of both husband and wife). When the house was eventually sold, the proceeds should be divided equally between the husband and wife.

Note however that if the court lets one spouse stay on in the house until the children grow up, it is becoming fairly common now for it to impose a condition that the house must be sold earlier if that spouse remarries or cohabits with someone for a significant period.

Case 4

A couple had been married for about thirteen years when the husband left home to live with another woman. The wife went on living in the family home with their son. Apart from a small amount of capital that the wife had saved, the only asset that the couple had was the house. After the divorce, they agreed that it should be put into their joint names and that they should be entitled to half its value each when it was sold. They could not agree when the sale should take place. The wife wanted to stay in the house and continue to use it as her home whereas the husband wanted it to be sold so that he could realise his capital.

The court decided that the wife would be able to afford to buy alternative accommodation from her share in the proceeds of sale of the house, even if this meant a drop in living standards for her and therefore it decided that the house should be sold straightaway.

Case 5
After 14 years of marriage, a husband and wife separated. The wife remained in the family home which was in the husband's name, with the four children. By the time the Court considered the case, the husband was a police officer aged 49 and the wife a community nurse aged 44. Both were earning roughly the same, but the husband also got a police flat in which he could live rent free. Both husband and wife were eligible for a lump sum on retirement, but the husband stood to get considerably more than the wife and would receive his money at an earlier date than she would. The two eldest children, both boys, were over 18 and were in apprenticeships and able to contribute weekly sums to their mother. In the five years or so since the husband left, the wife had brought up the children, maintained the house and latterly met the mortgage repayments as well as doing a full time job.

The court felt that the wife was going to remain the centre of the family for some years to come, at least until all the children were married and/or settled on their own. She was in need of a home, whereas the husband showed no signs of moving out of the police flat until he left the force. Even then, he had employment prospects for another seven years or so. The court therefore decided that the house should be transferred to the wife who should be responsible for its upkeep and the mortgage. The husband would normally have had to maintain the two youngest children but, in view of the fact that he was losing all his share in the house, the court decided that he would not have to pay any maintenance for them (unless circumstances changed drastically to make this necessary). As the wife was earning nearly as much as her husband, she would not have been entitled to any maintenance whatever decision had been made over the house.

Case 6
After 16 years of marriage, a wife petitioned for divorce. The husband moved into lodgings and the wife stayed with the three children, aged between 11 and 15 in the family house which she and her husband owned jointly. The husband was earning roughly three times as much as the wife who was working part time. She had family allowance and other social security benefits. The wife wanted to go on bringing up the children in the house.

The court decided that the house should be transferred into the wife's name alone, within three months. Thereafter she would have to pay all the outgoings and the mortgage. If she died, or the property was sold, the husband would be entitled to 25% of the proceeds of sale. The husband would not have to pay any maintenance for his wife but would have to pay a weekly sum for each child.

Case 7
Shortly after they were married, the wife's father bought the husband and wife a farm which he eventually gave to the wife absolutely. The husband put a great deal of effort into improving the farm which was run down and built it up into a successful business which he and the wife ran as partners. They had three sons. When they were divorced, the husband had to leave the farm which was his only means of livelihood. He asked the court to order the wife to transfer part of the farm to him or pay him a lump sum of money so that he could, for example, set himself up as a tenant farmer. The wife's only means of livelihood was also the farm. When *the court* considered the case it decided that the wife had large needs – to maintain herself and the boys and to provide for the upkeep of their home and education. The husband on the other hand had only himself to look after but he did need a home, whereas the wife had a home at the farm. The most the wife could raise without having to sell the farm (which had been valued at over £100,000) was £15,000. The court decided that she should pay this to the husband in three instalments. They felt it would be wrong to force her to sell her livelihood by ordering a larger sum.

Case 8
The husband's family and he had acquired a hotel which he (and the wife) had made into an increasingly profitable business. The

husband also had, from his family, shares in four family companies which owned substantial assets. The total value of the husband's assets when the case was decided was £215,000 so he was a fairly wealthy man in those days. A substantial part of his wealth was however his share in the hotel business. There were three children.

The court investigated what the wife would reasonably need on the breakdown of the marriage. It decided she would need a house and enough money to meet the running expenses of it and of a car, and to buy food, and also a capital sum to put her in the position she would have been in had the marriage continued. The husband had said during the marriage that he intended to give her a share in the hotel. It was decided that the wife should receive a lump sum of £70,000 from the husband and also sums for her own maintenance and for the three children, including boarding school fees for the two boys.

PART IV: PRACTICAL CONSIDERATIONS IN RELATION TO THE COURT HEARING

1. Who can apply?

a) *Orders in relation to a husband or wife*
Either of you can apply for a financial provision or property adjustment order in your own favour. Husbands and wives are treated equally and it makes no difference whether you were the petitioner or the respondent in the divorce proceedings. In an appropriate case, you can both apply for orders in your own favour. For example, a wife might apply for maintenance and her husband might apply to have some of the family assets transferred to him.

b) *Orders in relation to the children*
Whichever spouse has custody of a child of the family can apply to the court for a financial provision or property adjustment on behalf of that child. In addition, the child himself can seek permission to apply for an order on his own behalf. For example, a twenty year old student was given leave to apply for maintenance from her parents.

2. When can the application be made?

Applications for long term financial provision or property

adjustment orders can generally be commenced as soon as divorce proceedings have been started. It is advisable to play safe and make all the claims that you think might be appropriate at an early stage. For this reason, most petitioners normally make a comprehensive selection of claims in their petition, and many respondents will find that their solicitor files a similar application on their behalf soon after the start of the divorce proceedings.

If you do not make an application before you remarry you will lose your right to apply for orders in your own favour, although not for the children (see Chapter 25). Even if you do not remarry, you can lose your rights to claim orders for yourself if you delay unduly after the divorce before making your application.

3. How soon will the court hear the case?

The court can deal with maintenance and lump sum orders for children at any time after the divorce proceedings have been commenced.

All other long term questions of financial provision and property adjustment will have to wait until after decree nisi of divorce has been pronounced. Once this has been done, the court can consider any outstanding claims to financial provision and property adjustment orders. (Note: see Chapter 20 as regards pressing financial difficulties before this stage can be reached).

It is often some time before the court can actually deal with applications. Exactly how long you will have to wait depends very much on how busy the court is and what your case involves. As a general rule, the more you are able to agree over, the quicker the court will be able to resolve your case finally. If there is a lot of evidence to be gathered for the hearing or if your case involves a great deal of complex issues, it can take weeks or even months before the court can consider the case and give a final decision.

Even if the court does manage to decide your case before your divorce decree is made absolute, the orders that it makes will not come into effect until decree absolute of divorce is granted.

4. What will happen at the hearing?

Normally there will be one hearing to deal with all the financial and property issues in your case, whether they concern the children or yourselves. Prior to the hearing, you and your spouse will be asked to swear affidavits setting out in writing your income, capital and outgoings and outlining the claims you are making to the court. Copies of your affidavits will be exchanged between you and copies provided for the court. This written evidence will usually form the basis of the court hearing.

Do not worry about the hearing or the preparation for it. This is a job for your solicitor – if you qualify financially for Legal Aid, you should be entitled to help with your solicitor's fees under the scheme (see Chapter 4). He will represent you at the hearing himself, or will arrange for a barrister to deal with the case for you if necessary.

The hearing itself will be held in the Registrar's chambers – his office at court. You will find it relatively informal. It is private and can be attended only by those people directly involved in the case (usually yourselves, your legal representatives and the Registrar). You will probably be asked to give evidence orally to the Registrar. You may also have to answer questions from your spouse's solicitor or barrister. Your solicitor will be given an opportunity to address the Registrar about your case on your behalf. The Registrar will then make up his mind what order should be made. The normal course is for him to announce his decision immediately, so you should know the outcome of the case by the time you leave the hearing. If, however, there is any delay at any stage in the proceedings and you are in urgent need of money to live on, the Registrar can be asked to make a temporary maintenance order known as an 'interim periodical payments order' just to tide you over until a final decision can be made.

22
Tax and Your Divorce

(All the examples given in this chapter are based upon the tax rules in force for the tax year April 1986 to April 1987. Tax rules are subject to change, particularly in the rates of tax and the amounts of personal tax reliefs. You should check on the current position before you decide what to do about your own affairs.)

Tax is probably the last thing you want to think about when you are in the throes of separation and divorce. Nevertheless, you should not ignore it when it comes to making arrangements about your property and finances. By careful planning it is sometimes possible for both of you to save quite substantial sums in tax.

This is not a book specialising in tax and a detailed account of tax law would be out of place. There are many helpful publications available from booksellers that deal with all the principles of personal taxation. This chapter gives an outline of tax considerations that are of particular importance to the average person going through a divorce.

It is not usually necessary to consult an accountant about most of the routine questions that arise when you separate or get divorced – you will find that your solicitor will be able to give you the advice you need on the best way to arrange your own financial affairs. However, if you or your spouse have a particularly large income or if you have a great deal of valuable assets, you may find that you need to enlist the services of an accountant as well.

I. THE BASIC TAX POSITION

1. What taxes are likely to affect me?
There are three taxes that are likely to affect most of us at some stage in our lives. They are income tax, inheritance tax (formerly known as capital transfer tax) and capital gains tax.

2. What do these taxes involve?

a) *Income tax:* everyone is familiar with income tax – the tax that you pay on whatever income you receive. For most of us, our major (or only) liability to income tax is on our earnings from our employment.

b) *Inheritance tax* (formerly known as capital transfer tax): this is potentially payable on the value of your money and property which passes on your death and on any money or property you have transferred within 7 years before your death. It has replaced capital transfer tax which used to be charged both on transfers of property on death and on lifetime transfers. You do not normally need to concern yourself with inheritance tax in connection with your divorce.

c) *Capital gains tax (CGT):* this is payable on capital gains that you make when you dispose of property during your lifetime. 'Disposing' of property includes not only selling it but also giving it away. So you may be liable for CGT even though you never receive the money that represents the gain in value that may have accrued between the time you acquired the property and the time when you give it away.

Although CGT is payable on disposals of most types of property, it is not payable when you give away money (sterling). There are also other exemptions from CGT, for example you are permitted to make modest gains each year free of CGT (presently £5,900 per annum) and you may also make tax free gains on the disposal of certain items, for example your car or your home. Further rules make capital *losses* allowable against gains before tax is charged. Advice may be sought if you are facing problems.

As an example of the way that tax operates in the case of a simple single gain, let us suppose that Tom buys an antique in 1980 for £10,000. In 1985, he sells it for £20,000. He has made a gain of £10,000 and he will have to pay CGT on the gain unless he can show that the disposal comes within the exceptions to the tax.

Even if Tom had given away the antique, tax could have been payable. Suppose that he gave it to his goddaughter, Susan in 1985. He would be liable to CGT on the theoretical £10,000 gain. As for Susan, she would acquire the antique (it would be assumed) for £20,000, and if in due course she came to dispose of it herself, she would have to pay tax on any gain she made over this figure.

However, where an item is *given* away, the giver and the recipient can agree to make a claim to the Inland Revenue to postpone the payment of CGT. If Tom and his goddaughter had made such a claim, Tom would not have had to pay any CGT on the gift. However, Susan would be assumed to have acquired the antique from Tom at its value in 1985 less the gain that Tom had made (£20,000–£10,000) i.e. £10,000. This means that when she came to dispose of the antique in the future her CGT would be assessed as the difference between £10,000 and whatever she got for the antique. It would therefore lead to a larger tax bill than if she had acquired the antique in the normal way with Tom paying the CGT due. This procedure is known as 'holding over' or 'rolling over' the gain. The actual figures are more complex than as shown above, because there is relief for inflation which has occurred since the mid 1980's.

II. THE TAX POSITION WHILST YOU AND YOUR SPOUSE ARE LIVING TOGETHER AS MAN AND WIFE

In order to understand how separation and divorce may affect your tax position, you must have a general grasp of how tax is imposed on you during your marriage. This section therefore deals with the tax position whilst you and your spouse are living together.

a) *Income tax:* everyone is entitled to a certain amount of tax free income each year – this is called a 'personal relief'. The amount of personal relief to which you are entitled varies according to your circumstances (whether you are single, married etc.). The amounts are fixed by Parliament each year as a result of the Budget, and the examples below are based on 1986/7 rates.

Whilst a couple are married and living together, the husband usually gets a married man's personal relief (£3,655). He can also claim relief for his wife's earned income (up to a maximum of £2,335). The maximum wife's earned income relief is equal to the personal relief that is available to all single people. In the normal way, the income of husband and wife is added together and treated for tax purposes as one single income. The husband is liable to pay any tax due.

If you have relatively high earnings it may pay to do a few sums because you are entitled to be *taxed separately* as if you were two single people. You are then both allowed a single person's relief but you lose the married man's relief and wife's earned income relief that you would otherwise have had. As you can see, this means that you are allowed to receive less tax free income than if you had opted for taxation as a married couple in the normal way (you will now be allowed to receive only £4,670 tax free, whereas if you were taxed as a married couple you could have received £5,990 tax free). However it may be worth it to you to forgo this advantage because, as single people, the income tax that you pay on your individual earnings may be assessed at a lower rate than you would have paid in the aggregate if your earnings had been added together. This is because each individual taxpayer is allowed to receive a limited amount of income (up to £17,200) on which he pays tax only at 'basic rate', that is the lowest rate for the time being in force. Once this limit is exceeded, any further income that that taxpayer receives is taxed at progressively higher rates. By electing to be taxed as two single taxpayers, you ensure that you are allowed to receive two portions of earnings (£34,400 in total) on which tax is only payable at basic rate, whereas if you had been taxed in the normal way as a couple, you would have been allowed to receive only one portion of income (£17,200) taxed at basic rate.

Even if you do not wish to be taxed separately (and it is a disadvantage to elect separate taxation if your earnings are not sufficiently high) you may each want to deal with the Inland Revenue separately. People want to do this for a variety of reasons, for example some do not think it fair that the husband should receive the tax bill for his wife's earnings, or a wife may prefer to keep the details of her financial situation private from her husband. If you would prefer to deal with your own tax position in this way, you can notify the Inland Revenue that you wish to do so, and they will ensure that you are *assessed separately* for income tax.

Do not confuse separate assessment with separate taxation. Unlike the situation when you elect to be taxed separately, the amount that you pay between you will *not* be affected in any way by separate assessment – it is still worked out as if you were being taxed as a married couple in the normal way, and you can continue to take advantage of the married man's relief and wife's earned income relief. But you are each responsible for your own tax return and for any other dealings that you may have with the Inland Revenue over income tax. You are each liable to pay the amount of tax that relates to your share of the income yourself. The personal reliefs that you are entitled to as a couple will be shared between you.

b) *Capital Gains Tax (CGT):* normally the husband is responsible for any tax payable on capital gains made by either one of a married couple who are living together. As a married couple you are allowed to make, between you, only the same amount of tax free capital gains each year as if you were one single individual. If you prefer to deal separately with the Inland Revenue in relation to CGT, you can do so just as you can in relation to income tax. You have to make a separate decision in relation to each tax – you will not automatically be assessed separately for capital gains tax simply because you have elected this for income tax. However even if you do make the choice to be assessed separately, the amount of CGT you pay between you will not be affected. It is not possible to reduce the amount to be paid in tax on capital gains by being assessed separately as it is with income tax.

Whilst you are living together as husband and wife, you can

make disposals of property to each other without incurring any capital gains tax. When one spouse (say the husband) disposes of property to the other spouse, she simply steps into his shoes as if she had originally acquired the property when he did. This means that no capital gains tax is payable at this stage. However, when the wife comes to dispose of the property at a later date, to anyone other than her husband, she will usually have to pay tax on a gain that is greater than the gain on which she would have had to pay tax if capital gains tax had been paid at the earlier stage on the gain that had accrued so far.

To return to Tom, let us suppose that he gave the antique which he bought for £10,000 to his wife, Cheryl, in 1985 when it was worth £20,000. Neither Tom nor Cheryl would have to pay any tax on the gain of £10,000 that had been made so far, although this might have been taxed had they not been married. If Cheryl then sells the antique to a dealer in 1990 for £26,000, she will have to pay tax as if she had originally acquired the antique back in 1980 when Tom actually bought it. So she will have to pay tax on a gain of £16,000 (the original purchase price of £10,000 deducted from the selling price of £26,000) whereas if she and Tom were not husband and wife and the capital gains tax had been paid in 1985 on the £10,000 gain that had accrued so far, she would only have to pay tax for the £6,000 gain that had been made between 1985 and 1990, less indexation allowance.

III. THE TAX POSITION IF YOU START TO LIVE APART

Will separation affect my tax position?
The simple answer is yes, your tax position in relation to income tax and capital gains tax will be affected if you live apart from your spouse.

What counts as living apart?
You are living apart for tax purposes if:

a) you are separated under a court order or a deed of separation; or

b) you are separated in such circumstances that your separation is likely to be permanent.

How is living apart likely to affect my tax position?
a) *Income tax:* the Inland Revenue only look upon you as a married couple as long as you are living together. As soon as you separate therefore, both your tax positions will alter. It is not

usually possible to revert to the tax position of a single individual at once, so there are special rules for the tax year in which you actually separate. This means that (unless you have elected separate taxation at some stage before you actually separated) the income you receive for the period before your separation is added together in the normal way and you are taxed on this as a married couple. The husband can claim a married man's relief and a full wife's earned income relief for this part of the year. Income that you each receive after you separate will be taxed individually. The wife becomes entitled to her own single person's relief for the period after the separation and her husband cannot therefore claim any wife's earned income relief for this period. However, although strictly speaking he is now looked upon as a single man, he is permitted to claim his whole married man's relief for the remainder of the year of separation.

If the wife has any of the children living with her who are under 16, or over 16 and still undergoing full time education at school or university etc., or who are undergoing at least a two year course of training for a trade, profession or vocation, she may be able to claim an additional personal relief (an additional sum of £1,320 to bring her personal relief up to the amount allowed for a married man) for the remainder of the year after the separation.

After the end of the tax year in which you separate, the long term position is as follows:–

i) you are both taxed as individuals on your own earned and unearned income. You are each responsible to the Inland Revenue in respect of your own tax, both for making returns and for paying any amount due.

ii) you both get only a single person's relief (except that, until you are actually divorced, a husband can go on claiming a married man's personal relief if he wholly maintains his wife by voluntary payments – see later in this chapter page 164).

iii) either one of you (or both) may be able to claim the additional personal relief mentioned above if you are looking after one or more of the children. You cannot claim this additional relief if you are already claiming a married man's personal relief.

b) *Capital Gains Tax:* as soon as you separate, you will revert to the status of single people for capital gains tax. This means that:–

i) you each pay capital gains tax on your own gains.

ii) you are each allowed your own portion of tax free gains

each year (that means that between you you will be able to make double the amount that you were allowed to make tax free as a couple).

iii) after the end of the tax year in which you separate, the position in relation to CGT on disposals between spouses alters and you may have to pay tax on any gain that you make when you dispose of property to your spouse. However, you may be able to claim to hold over any gain you make in this way (see earlier in this chapter at page 158).

IV. TAX ON AND AFTER THE DIVORCE

What counts as a divorce for tax purposes?
A divorce is only of consequence from the tax point of view once decree nisi has been made absolute.

Will divorce change my tax position further?

a) *Income tax:* most of the income tax changes that result from your marriage breaking down occur when you separate. Of course, if you only separate on divorce, rather than before, these tax changes will coincide with the divorce. Once you are divorced you cannot be taxed as a couple, even if you go on living together for some reason. Furthermore, even if the husband goes on wholly maintaining his wife from voluntary payments, he will not be able to claim a married man's personal relief after the divorce.

b) *Capital Gains Tax:* as with income tax, the major tax changes arise when you separate rather than as a result of the divorce. Once the divorce comes through, you will not be treated as a couple for CGT even if you continue living together for some reason.

V. MATTERS THAT REQUIRE SPECIAL CONSIDERATION

1. Income tax and maintenance payments
It is most important to consider tax when you decide how you are going to pay (or receive) maintenance. By making prudent arrangements, you could save yourselves a worthwhile sum in tax.

There are basically three alternative ways to provide maintenance for your spouse or children. These are:

a) by making voluntary payments

b) by undertaking a binding obligation to make payments by means of a separation deed, maintenance agreement, covenant etc.

c) by making payments under a court order.

As it is far more common for a husband to make maintenance payments for his wife and children rather than for a wife to make provision for her husband or children, the advice that follows is addressed to the husband as payer and the wife as recipient of maintenance payments. However, if, in your case, the wife will be making maintenance payments, you will find that, for the most part, the same principles apply.

This section deals only with the tax side of things – for advice on other practical advantages and disadvantages of each method of payment you should refer to Chapter 18.

Payments to your wife

a) *Voluntary payments*

You are treated as making voluntary payments if, although you do actually pay maintenance, you are not legally bound to do so, by a separation deed or firm binding oral agreement or by a court order. If you choose to make maintenance payments in this way, your own and your wife's tax positions will be largely unaffected by the payments. The arrangement will work like this:–

i) you pay your wife whatever you think fit from your own income;

ii) you do not get any tax relief for what you pay;

iii) but you may be entitled to one concession as a result of your arrangement – whereas, after the end of the tax year in which you separate you would normally only be able to claim a single person's personal relief, if you wholly maintain your wife by your voluntary payments, you will be allowed to go on claiming a married man's personal relief instead;

iv) your wife receives the money that you pay her just as if she was getting housekeeping money from you in the normal way – she does not have to pay tax on what you give her.

Take the case of Betty and Arthur. When they separate they do not give any thought to the question of maintenance for Betty for the future. However, as it is some time before they can get divorced, Arthur decides that during their separation he will voluntarily pay Betty £3,120 a year (£60 a week) by way of maintenance. This is Betty's only source of income. Arthur pays

Betty the £60 a week out of his pay packet just as he used to give her housekeeping whilst they were living together.

He can as explained go on claiming the married man's personal relief as he did when they were living together because he is wholly maintaining Betty by means of his voluntary payments, although he will no longer be able to claim the larger allowance once they are divorced. This means that because of his payments to Betty, Arthur receives an additional £1,320 of his income tax free each year because his personal relief is increased from £2,335 to £3,655.

Even though Betty may have had to pay some tax on ordinary earnings of £60 per week, because Arthur pays her voluntarily she does not have to pay any tax on what she receives from him. She can use the full £60 each week for her own requirements.

Although this may seem to be a fairly simple way of arranging your maintenance payments, it is not usually the cheapest method of providing for your wife, as you will see from the alternatives outlined below. This is because you do not get tax relief for the maintenance payments you make in this way – the most you can get is an increased personal allowance.

b) *Payments under a maintenance agreement or other binding obligation*

Even if there is no court order in force in your case, it is quite possible to put your own arrangements for maintenance on a formal footing by undertaking a binding obligation to pay maintenance to your wife. This can be done in a variety of ways, for example, you and your wife could enter into a maintenance agreement or a separation deed could be drawn up including provision for maintenance (see Chapter 18). It is possible to make a binding agreement over maintenance by word of mouth, but it is not usually wise to do so – oral agreements can lead to disputes in the future over exactly what was agreed between you and it can be difficult to satisfy the Inland Revenue that you really do have a binding obligation to make maintenance payments so that they will allow you to claim tax relief on them. There are certain rules that must be observed even with a written agreement to make sure that it is binding on you, and it is always a good idea to consult your solicitor at an early stage over any arrangement that you propose to make so that he can approve it and put it in writing for you in a suitable form.

If you make a legally binding arrangement to pay your wife (before or after divorce) a recurring sum by way of maintenance (for example £100 monthly or £50 per week or one third of your income each week) for a period that can exceed a year, it will have the following effect on your own and your wife's tax position:–

i) you will get tax relief from all rates of tax for the sum you undertake to pay;

ii) you will only be able to claim a single person's personal allowance instead of a married man's allowance, even though you may not yet be divorced;

iii) the sum you have undertaken to pay will form part of your wife's income for tax purposes and she can be liable to pay income tax at the appropriate rate on it. The appropriate rate is calculated according to her own personal circumstances – how much maintenance you have undertaken to pay, what income she receives from other sources, what personal relief she is entitled to etc.

What actually happens in practice is that, whenever you make a payment of maintenance to your wife, you withhold part of the sum you have undertaken to pay. You calculate how much you should keep back by working out how much income tax would be payable on the whole sum that you have undertaken to pay at the basic rate of tax. So for example, if you have undertaken to pay your wife £100 a month and the basic rate of tax for the time being is 29%, you keep back £29 each month and pay your wife only £71. Normally you can then keep the sum that you have withheld so that each £1 of maintenance you have undertaken to pay will only, in fact, cost you 71 pence – in this way you are giving yourself tax relief from basic rate tax on the amount you have agreed to pay to your wife. In the rare cases where you do not have to pay any income tax or you pay less tax on your total income than the sum you have withheld from your wife, you will have to pay some or all of the money you have kept back to the Inland Revenue. This is because you cannot have tax relief unless you were liable to pay tax in the first place.

If you pay tax at higher rates, you get tax relief from this by arrangement between you and the Inland Revenue through the PAYE system or by means of a tax rebate, rather than by adjusting your payment to your wife any more than to offset the basic rate.

It is most important to remember to deduct the appropriate sum when you make maintenance payments to your wife; if you do not do so, you may find that you have lost your tax relief.

You have an obligation to your wife to provide her

periodically with a certificate showing how much maintenance you have withheld so that she can sort out her own tax position with the Inland Revenue. As you will see, the amount you have withheld from your wife is in fact treated as tax paid by her, so the certificate that you provide will in fact be showing the tax you have deducted on your wife's behalf. (Blank forms of the certificate used are available from the Inland Revenue.)

Your wife receives less maintenance in spending terms than you undertook to pay her. Nevertheless, the whole sum that was originally agreed is treated as part of her income for tax purposes. So if you agree to pay her £100 a month, she in fact receives only £71 per month but her liability to income tax will be assessed as if she had received the whole £100. The Inland Revenue then look upon the sum that you withheld as tax paid by your wife on her maintenance. So, in this example, she is treated as already having paid £29 tax on the maintenance of £100 to which she was entitled. This means that, if her tax bill works out so that she is liable for basic rate tax on the maintenance, she will not have to make any further income tax payments on it: her tax bill is automatically satisfied by the amount you deducted before you handed over the maintenance.

It can work out however, that your wife is not liable to any tax or is liable to less tax than you have deducted from the payments you made, perhaps because the total income she receives is less than her personal relief. If so, she has paid more tax than she owes and she is entitled to reclaim the excess from the Inland Revenue. Normally repayments are made annually but she can arrange more frequent repayments (for example quarterly) with the Inland Revenue if it would cause her hardship to wait longer. If on the other hand, your wife has a substantial income and is liable for higher rates of income tax on the maintenance, she will have to pay the extra tax (over and above the tax at basic rate which she is deemed to have paid already).

To return to Arthur and Betty, let us suppose that they now give rather more thought to the question of maintenance and decide to enter into a maintenance agreement. Their solicitor draws up an agreement for them whereby they both agree to various things, one being that Arthur will pay Betty £3,120 each year by way of maintenance. Because he is now legally bound to make the payment, Arthur can get tax relief for it. He will make the payment in the way described above. He deducts and keeps back from each instalment a sum equal to income tax at basic rate on that instalment. So, if he pays Betty maintenance weekly, she would be entitled to a weekly sum of £60 under the agreement but Arthur would deduct £17.40 each week and pay her only £42.60 (basic rate of tax = 29%). Arthur is a modest earner and has no other source of income other than his job, so he does not have to worry about higher rates of tax, but if he did, he would get tax relief from this by arrangement with the Inland Revenue – he would still pay Betty £42.60 each week. The higher the rate of tax for which Arthur was liable, the cheaper the maintenance would be for him, so if he paid tax at 50%, each £1 of maintenance that he paid to Betty would ultimately only cost him 50 pence when his tax position had been adjusted. As for Betty, she is treated as if she had received the full £60 each week and paid basic rate tax on it herself of £17.40. She is entitled to a single person's personal relief of £2,335 and is in fact only liable to pay tax on any income that she receives in excess of this amount. As the maintenance is her only source of income, she is therefore only liable to pay tax on £785 of the maintenance (£3,120 minus £2,335). She has actually paid tax on the whole £3,120 and she will therefore be able to reclaim a substantial proportion of the tax that Arthur deducted from the Inland Revenue. Like Arthur, she has no worries about higher rates of tax, but if she had had a big income and was liable for higher rates of tax, she would have had to pay the extra tax due on the maintenance payment herself.

If you compare this arrangement to the original voluntary maintenance that Arthur was paying to Betty, you will see that Arthur has exchanged the married man's personal relief that he was drawing then for a single person's relief, thus losing £1,320 of tax free income. Instead he can obtain tax relief for £3,120 of maintenance. Betty has to pay a price for this as she will have suffered a small amount of tax on the maintenance even after she has reclaimed some of the money that Arthur deducted from the Inland Revenue. Arthur and Betty should be able to adjust their agreement so that Arthur can agree to pay Betty slightly more maintenance to compensate her for the tax she will suffer; he should be able to do this comfortably because of the increased tax relief to which he is entitled.

It is possible to make your undertaking to pay maintenance to your wife in such a way that she will always receive the same amount of money from you no matter what the basic rate of tax in force. The exact wording of the undertaking is important. If you wish to come to this sort of arrangement, you should ask your solicitor to advise you as to how it would affect you and, if he feels it would be appropriate, to draft a suitable form of undertaking for you.

c) *Payments under a court order*
If you are ordered by the court to make maintenance payments to your wife, your tax position will depend on the amount of the payments.

(i) Small maintenance payments: if you are ordered to pay only a small amount of maintenance (at present, up to and including £48 per week) at weekly or monthly intervals, you will still get tax relief for your maintenance payments, but the method by which you make the payments will be different from that described in the last section. You simply pay the whole of the amount ordered without making any deductions first. You get your tax relief through the PAYE system or by claiming a rebate from the Inland Revenue instead of by depriving your wife of part of her maintenance.

Your wife declares what she receives as part of her income and is liable to pay tax on it at whatever rate is appropriate to her personal circumstances. If her income does not exceed her personal relief, she will not have to pay any tax on the maintenance and she is saved the bother of having to reclaim tax from the Inland Revenue. However, she may have to pay basic and higher rates of tax on the maintenance if her circumstances warrant this.

You can only use this method of payment if a court orders you to make small maintenance payments. If you are paying under any other binding obligation, you will have to deduct tax before you make each payment as described earlier, even if the amount you have undertaken to pay is within the small maintenance limits.

(ii) Larger maintenance payments:– an order for maintenance payments that exceed the limit of a small maintenance order will have exactly the same effect as the binding obligation described in the last section. So, to get basic rate tax relief on the amount of maintenance ordered, you make the payments to your wife after deducting tax at basic rate. If you are liable to higher rates of tax, you get further tax relief through the PAYE system or by tax rebate. You provide your wife with certificates showing how much tax you have deducted. She receives the amount ordered less the tax and her tax position is then adjusted if necessary with the Inland Revenue by a repayment of any overpaid tax or by her accounting to the Inland Revenue for any extra tax due if she pays higher rates of tax.

Payments to or for your children

Every child, whatever his age, is taxed as a single person. He is permitted to receive his own share of tax free income up to the limit of a single person's personal relief. Normally you should, if possible, ensure that you pay maintenance direct to your child so that it becomes his income instead of yours. Provided that you do not pay him more than his personal relief, he will not have to pay any tax on the maintenance. Even if the payments do exceed his personal relief, it is likely that his tax bill on the maintenance will still be less than your own or your wife's would have been on the equivalent sum. How you should pay maintenance for your child to get the best tax advantage will depend on his age.

a) UNMARRIED CHILDREN UNDER 18

i) *Where there is no court order for the payment of maintenance*

Even if you undertake a binding obligation to pay maintenance to your child, the sum you pay will still be treated as your own income rather than his. This is uneconomical because it means that you do not get any tax relief for the payments and the child's personal relief may well be wasted. The way round this is to increase the amount that you are obliged to pay to your wife so that it, in fact, includes a sum for your child. As you have seen the full amount that you pay to your wife will qualify for tax relief. However, to make this arrangement effective, you must be very careful not to refer in the maintenance agreement, separation deed etc., to the fact that part of the money is earmarked for your child's benefit – if you do, all the tax advantage will be lost. Even this method of payment, however, does not make use of your child's own personal relief because it is your wife who is taxed on the income that you pay for the child's benefit, not the child himself. The only way to ensure that your child is the one who is taxed on the payment is to have your obligation to pay maintenance to him embodied in a court order.

ii) *Payments under a court order*

If you are ordered by the court to make maintenance payments *to your child*, you will get full tax relief for the payments and your child may be taxed on the amount of the maintenance. How this is accomplished in practice, depends on the amount you are ordered to pay. If you are ordered to pay a sum .nat is payable at weekly or montly intervals and does not exceed £48 per week in the case of payments ordered to be made *to* the child or £25 per week in the case of payments ordered to be made *to any other person for the benefit of the child* it is classed as a *small maintenance payment*. This means that you hand over the whole sum that you are ordered to pay to the child. You are given tax relief from all rates of tax by arrangement with the Inland Revenue through the PAYE system or by claiming a rebate. Your child has to pay tax on the income if his personal circumstances warrant this. If he gets no income from other sources, his income from you will not exceed his personal relief and he will have no tax to pay.

If you are ordered to pay more than £48/£25 per week, you will find that the order works in exactly the same way as an order to pay larger sums of maintenance to your wife or a binding obligation to make maintenance payments to her. So you are obliged to make your payments after deducting tax at basic rate. You get tax relief from higher rates of tax by adjustment with the Inland Revenue. Your child can reclaim any overpaid tax if you have deducted more than the tax for which he is actually liable, or must pay any further tax for which he is liable to the Inland Revenue. Full use is thus made of your child's personal relief.

Although the order requires payment to the child, it is usually possible to make the actual payment to a third party, say your wife, for the child.

If on the other hand, your court order provides for payments to be made *to your wife for the maintenance of the child*, the payments will be treated in exactly the same way as any maintenance ordered to be paid to her for her own benefit – you get tax relief but the payments form part of your wife's income, not the child's.

b) OLDER OR MARRIED CHILDREN

i) *Payment without a court order*

You can get tax relief for payments that you make from basic rate tax only provided that you undertake a binding obligation to make the payments (for example by entering into a maintenance agreement including a provision that you will pay maintenance to the child or a covenant to pay). You should normally ensure that you are obliged to pay for a period that could exceed six years or the arrangement will not be effective to give you any tax relief, nor will the income be treated as your child's income; it will remain yours for all purposes. If you are contemplating an arrangement of this kind you should ask your solicitor for help.

ii) *Payments under a court order*
It is possible for the court to make an order for the payment of maintenance to a child who is 18 or over, provided that the child is or will be receiving education or training or there are other special factors in your case (see Chapter 21). An order of this type will normally have exactly the same effect as a similar order for a younger child.

There are other methods of providing maintenance for your child, for example, if you have the resources you could set up a trust for him. These alternative methods usually require careful planning and it is outside the scope of this book to deal with them. If you feel you might like to consider other ways in which to maintain your child, you should mention this to your solicitor.

GETTING A COURT ORDER
As you can see, it is often advantageous to have your obligation to pay maintenance for your family declared in a court order. You should refer to Chapter 21 for details of the court orders that can be made. One cannot normally apply for a divorce court order against oneself, in other words you will not usually be able to ask the divorce court to order you to pay maintenance to a member of your family yourself. However, your wife will almost certainly have made claims for maintenance in her petition if she began the divorce proceedings and, if you are agreed over the amount of maintenance that is to be paid, your solicitor will normally be able to arrange with her for this to be put into a court order. If you began the divorce proceedings it will still normally be possible for your wife to make claims for maintenance that will enable the court to make the order that you want.

2. Meeting expenses for your family

a) *School fees*
There are various alternative methods of meeting your child's school fees after a separation or divorce; a few are listed here:–

i) You could simply go on paying the school fees voluntarily direct to the school as you have probably always done. You will get no tax relief for the fees if you do this and you may be wasting tax advantage from which you could otherwise benefit.

ii) You could increase the amount of maintenance that you are bound to pay to your wife so that she can meet the school fees. Provided that you do not refer in your agreement to the fact that the money is destined for your child's benefit or for the school fees, you will get tax relief for the money that you pay to your wife, but she will be taxed on it according to her own personal circumstances – it forms part of her maintenance in the normal way.

iii) If your child is an adult or married, you could make a covenant to pay your child an amount that will cover the costs. The covenant must be capable of lasting at least 6 years. It will then ensure that you get tax relief from basic rate tax for the payments that you make and that the income will form part of your child's income for tax purposes.

iv) Probably the best tax advantage will be obtained if your child makes an agreement with the school that he will pay the fees and a court order is made obliging you to pay the school fees to your child so that he can pay the school, or binding you to pay the fees direct to the school on the child's behalf. This type of order works just like an ordinary court order for maintenance to be paid to the child and gives you full relief from tax on the payments which form part of your child's income.

v) There are other arrangements possible for paying the school fees from income, and there are, of course, various schemes in existence that enable you to provide for the fees out of capital. Ask your solicitor or accountant for details if you feel you need to look into more alternatives.

b) *Other expenses such as rates, rent, heating bills etc.*
Be careful about agreeing to maintain your family partly or wholly by paying their bills. This can be wasteful of tax advantages that you could otherwise obtain. As a general rule, you will not get tax relief if you pay bills direct, whereas if you were to pay your spouse sufficient to meet the bills, this would be part of her maintenance and you would get tax relief on it, providing the payments were not made purely voluntarily. However, it may be all right to pay the mortgage interest for your wife – see the next section.

3. Getting maximum tax relief on your mortgage interest

You can obtain tax relief on interest that you pay on a loan of up to £30,000 taken out to buy or improve your only or main home. You probably took advantage of this when you were living with your spouse if you were buying your home with a mortgage. Of course, if you move out of the house when your marriage breaks down or on divorce, the house will no longer qualify as your own home. Nevertheless, if you retain a share in the house and go on making the mortgage repayments, you will still be able to claim income tax relief for the interest that you pay, provided that the house continues to be your spouse's (or former spouse's) main home.

This is all very well as long as you do not take out another loan to purchase new accommodation for yourself. If you do, you may well wish to claim tax relief on the interest that you pay on that loan too. It is possible to claim tax relief on loans on two houses in this way but, if the total of this loan and the one on your spouse's home comes to more than £30,000, you will not be able to claim relief on the interest on the excess over £30,000. This problem can often be overcome by arranging for the mortgage repayments to be made in a slightly different way.

When you and your spouse are separated or divorced, you are each eligible for your own tax relief on £30,000 worth of loans. It may therefore be better from the tax point of view for your spouse to make the mortgage repayments on the house in which she lives and for you to go on making the payments in respect of your own property. In this way you will both be able to claim tax relief on interest paid on loans of up to £30,000 giving you a total of £60,000 in all. To make this arrangement possible, it may be necessary for you to pay your wife extra by way of maintenance. As you have seen, you can get tax relief on maintenance that you pay if it is arranged in the right way. The net result of an arrangement of this sort could therefore be that, in fact, you get tax relief on all the interest that you pay on loans in relation to both homes even though the total amount borrowed exceeds £30,000. If you think that this sort of arrangement could help you, check with your solicitor whether it is feasible in your case and take his advice as to how it should be accomplished.

If you take out a mortgage (or a further mortgage) on your home to pay your spouse a lump sum as part of the divorce settlement, any interest on this mortgage may also qualify for tax relief provided you are using it to buy yourself an increased share in the house from your spouse.

4. Will either of us have to pay any Capital Gains tax as a result of sharing out our property on separation or divorce?

Separation or divorce will normally involve some redistribution of your family's assets, for example, you may take the car that is partly owned by your wife and she might keep all the furniture that you have acquired jointly over the years, or you may be ordered by the court to transfer the house from your own name into your wife's name.

Until you separate (and in the year of your separation) you can make whatever reallocation of assets between the two of you that you like without any immediate liability to CGT (see page 162). *After you separate* and the year is up, gains that you make on transferring property to your spouse could be chargeable to CGT depending on the type of property involved. However, it may still be possible to postpone the payment of tax until a later date if you both agree by claiming to hold over the gain (see page 158). When you dispose of your house to your spouse (or former spouse) it is often possible to escape entirely from CGT. This is because any gain which one makes when disposing of a property that was one's main home is exempt from CGT provided that one has not been absent from it for more than 2 years and that no other house has replaced it as one's main residence. Even if you have moved out more than two years ago, you may still escape CGT if you transfer an interest in the house to your spouse as part of a financial settlement on divorce or separation, provided your spouse has continued to occupy the house as her only or main residence and you have not elected to have any other property treated as your main residence.

23 Enforcing Agreements and Court Orders Dealing with Property and Finances

What do you do if your husband or wife tries to shirk his or her responsibilities towards you under an agreement you have made or under an order of the court? When problems do arise, they are generally over maintenance. One spouse fails to pay what he has agreed to pay or been ordered to pay by the court, or, if he does pay, his payments are sporadic or always late or rarely for the full amount. It is with this type of difficulty that this chapter deals.

Problems do sometimes arise over arrangements in respect of property. For example, the court orders the husband to transfer the house to his wife and he refuses to do so. The courts have machinery for ensuring that agreements made between spouses and its own orders are complied with. A special application to the court is required and your solicitor will advise and help you should you find yourself in difficulties of this kind. Just to give you an example of the sort of thing the court can do, to cope with the problem of the husband who refuses to transfer the house to his wife, the court could arrange for the house to be transferred without his consent.

1. Enforcing agreements about maintenance

You may have come to a formal agreement with your spouse about maintenance (see Chapter 18). If your spouse then fails to pay as he promised, you can take him to court for breaking the agreement. The court can then order him to pay you damages amounting to the arrears that have accumulated under the maintenance agreement. Each time fresh arrears accumulate, you will have to take your spouse back to court.

2. Enforcing maintenance orders made by the court.

In many cases, the court will make a maintenance order in favour of one spouse, or in favour of the children, on divorce. If your spouse then fails to pay in accordance with the order, you can take steps to enforce it. The exact method of enforcing the order will depend on whether it has been registered in the Magistrates' Court.

a) *If the order has been registered in the Magistrates' Court*

If your solicitor foresaw any problems with your maintenance, he may well have asked for permission to register the Divorce Court's maintenance order in the Magistrates' Court. This means that your spouse makes the maintenance payments under the court order to the Magistrates' Court office. They keep a record of what he has paid and pass the money on to you. If your spouse fails to pay, it is up to the Magistrates' clerk at your request to chase him up and, if necessary, bring him back to court (this time in front of the Magistrates) so that the situation can be remedied.

There are a number of ways in which the Magistrates can deal with the situation. For example:

(i) they can decide that your spouse should be excused from some or all of the arrears that have accumulated. They will then 'remit' or wipe out the appropriate amount of the arrears. Your spouse will, however, remain liable to pay your maintenance in the future, unless he asks, successfully, for the maintenance order to be reduced or terminated.

(ii) they can make arrangements for your spouse to pay off the arrears in instalments along with your current maintenance.

(iii) they can make an attachment of earnings order. This can be particularly effective in securing your maintenance for you in the future. It is addressed to your spouse's employer and directs him to deduct the amount of your maintenance from your spouse's wages or salary before he is paid. The employer then hands the money over to the court who make the payment of the maintenance to you.

(iv) if all else fails, they can send your spouse to prison for failing to pay your maintenance.

If you receive regular payments of supplementary benefit (because the amount of your maintenance order is less than the supplementary benefit limit or because your spouse is a bad payer), you may find it more convenient to make over your maintenance order to the Department of Health and Social Security. Under this arrangement, you authorise the court to pay the sums your spouse pays into the court office to the D.H.S.S. instead of to you. You are then entitled to draw your full supplementary benefit irrespective of what your spouse has paid.

b) *If the order is not registered in the Magistrates' Court*

If your order is not registered in the Magistrates' Court it is up to you to take your spouse back before the court that made the order in the first place if he fails to pay. The court will then be able to deal with the situation in a variety of ways, many of which are very similar to the remedies available in the Magistrates' Court. As *you* will have to prove that your spouse is in arrears with his payments, it is essential that you keep a clear and accurate record of the payments that he has made.

3. If your spouse goes abroad

What do you do if your spouse goes abroad and stops paying you the maintenance to which you are entitled? The courts of this country generally find it hard to enforce orders if the payer and his assets are no longer in the country. Therefore arrangements have been made with a large number of countries whereby maintenance orders can be transmitted abroad and enforced in the country where the payer happens to be.

You will certainly need legal help if you face this type of problem.

24
Varying Your Financial Arrangements at a Later Date

As you have seen from the preceding chapters, it is possible to put your financial arrangements on a formal basis in two ways – by entering into an agreement with your spouse or by asking the court to make an order dealing with your property and finances. Whichever way you choose, there may come a time when the arrangements you originally made are no longer appropriate, often because the husband's salary goes up and the wife feels she is entitled to more maintenance from him or because he loses his job or takes on heavy financial responsibilites (such as a new wife!) and feels that his liability to the (first) wife should be reduced. The court does have power to vary your original arrangements in certain circumstances, on your application.

1. Varying an agreement

If you want the court to vary arrangements embodied in an agreement with your spouse, you should refer to Chapter 18 for details of the circumstances in which this may be possible.

2. Varying a divorce court order

Maintenance orders: you are more likely to require a change in the Divorce Court's maintenance order (be it for maintenance pending suit or periodical payments in respect of a spouse or a child) than in any other order it may make. The court can vary maintenance orders but you will have to make out a good case for the change you seek. The court will take into account all the circumstances of your case, including particularly any changes that have occurred since it made the order, in deciding whether to grant a variation. If your maintenance order has been registered in the Magistrates' Court (see Chapter 23), your application for a variation will be heard by the magistrates. In other cases, it will be heard by the court that made the order originally.

If your maintenance claim was dismissed by the court after your divorce (see page 140), you cannot subsequently re-apply for maintenance for yourself. However, the court always has power to hear applications for maintenance for children of the family.

Lump sum orders: if you were awarded or ordered to pay a lump sum in one instalment only, the court will not be able to alter this order at all on a subsequent application.

If the lump sum was to be paid in more than one instalment however, the court can vary the arrangements for payment.

Orders in relation to property: if the court made an order in relation to your property on your divorce (for example, it may have ordered your husband or wife to transfer the matrimonial home to you), neither of you can ask for this order to be altered at a later date. However, if the court granted you 'liberty to apply' or ordered a sale of some of your property when it made the order, you will be able to go back to the court for further assistance in actually putting the order into practice. For example, if the court ordered that one of you should sell the house within three months and divide the proceeds between you, and a buyer for the house cannot be found, it would be possible to apply to the court for advice as to how to proceed.

Legal advice

The Green Form scheme will assist with the cost of advice from a solicitor about a variation of your order provided that you qualify financially for help under the scheme. Legal Aid for fuller representation by a solicitor (for instance, at the court hearing) is not easy to obtain for variation applications unless an unusual or difficult point is involved.

Appeals

Do not confuse applications for a variation of an order of the type described in this chapter with appeals against orders of the court. To obtain a *variation* of your order you do not need to show that there was anything wrong with the original order, merely that it would be right to alter it in the light of the present circumstances; your application to the court can be made, in many cases, a substantial period of time after the original order. On the other hand, you have the right to *appeal* against an order of the court (whether it is in relation to maintenance, or property, or a lump sum) if you feel that you have been unfairly treated. Your appeal will be heard by a more senior court and will succeed if you establish that the original order was wrong for some reason. You have only a limited period, often a matter of days, in which to indicate that you wish to appeal.

PART 7: OTHER THINGS TO CONSIDER

25
Getting Married Again

You are not free to remarry until your divorce is made final by decree absolute (see Chapter 12). You will need to produce a copy of the decree absolute before you will be allowed to remarry. Whether you will be able to have the wedding ceremony in a church depends on the views of the clergyman concerned.

Remarriage can have an effect on your rights against your former spouse. In particular, you should bear in mind the following points:

1. When you remarry, you will cease to be entitled to receive any further *periodical payments* for yourself (although not for the children) from your spouse. However, any orders that have already been made in relation to your property and capital will not be affected. Nor will you necessarily preserve your right to periodical payments by simply co-habiting with your new partner rather than getting married - although your right to periodical payments is not *automatically* wiped out, you could lose part or all of your periodical payments at least during your co-habitation particularly if the court feels that your new partner is contributing towards your living expenses (see Chapter 21).

2. If your spouse continues to pay maintenance to you after you have remarried, thinking that he is still obliged to do so, he can apply to the court for an order that the money over-paid should be returned to him by you.

3. If the spouse who is responsible for paying periodical payments remarries, this will not end his liability to make the payments to his former spouse and children. He can only have his liability reduced or extinguished if he can show that his

circumstances have changed as a result of his remarriage so that it is no longer right to require him to go on paying at the previous rate. The court does not normally allow a spouse to ignore his obligations to his first family in favour of his new family, so it will usually be an uphill task for him to satisfy the court that his maintenance payments should be terminated or reduced.

4. Once you remarry, you are no longer entitled to start a claim for *property adjustment orders or for a lump sum*, (for example for a share in the former matrimonial home). However, if you have begun your claim before you remarry, you will be allowed to continue with it after remarriage. If you are thinking of remarriage, and your property has not yet been sorted out after your divorce, you should therefore check with your solicitor that the appropriate claims have been made on your behalf. If you were the petitioner in the divorce suit, you will probably find that all the claims you need were made automatically in your divorce petition. If not, your solicitor will be able to take the necessary steps to make the claims before you remarry. If you were the respondent in the divorce proceedings, your claim is unlikely to have been made automatically even though you may have mentioned something about property in your acknowledgement of service. Your solicitor may well have filed the necessary application form on your behalf already, but if he has not, he should be able to do so before you remarry.

5. If you have remarried or you have definite plans to do so by the time the court considers your property after the divorce, it can take your likely married circumstances into account in determining what share you should have of the assets of your former marriage. For example, a wife who is about to get married again to a very wealthy man will not require as much capital as a wife who is struggling to support herself on maintenance. If you are co-habitating with your new partner (although you have not yet married), and the relationship appears permanent, the joint circumstances of you and your partner may also be relevant to the court.

6. Your rights in relation to the children will generally be completely unaffected by your remarriage. However, in the unlikely event of your remarrying or associating closely with someone who is totally unsuitable to be in contact with your children, you may find that you are faced with an application by your spouse to the court for an order depriving you of custody or access to the children. If the court thinks the application is justified, it can grant it (see Chapters 15 and 16).

7. Remember that (re-)marriage revokes your will automatically, so consider making a new one.

26
Modifying Your Will

No doubt, during your marriage, you have been quite content that a large part of your property (your 'estate') should go to your spouse after your death. However, when your marriage breaks down, your attitude may well change. It is therefore a good idea to review the question of who will inherit your property at an early stage, in many cases even before decree absolute of divorce comes through.

1. If you have no will
If you die without making a will, you are said to have died 'intestate'. A series of rules is then applied to determine who should inherit your estate.

If you die intestate *before* decree absolute of divorce is granted, as a general rule, all your personal belongings such as jewellery, clothes and pictures, will pass to your spouse together with the lion's share in your remaining property such as money, land etc., (exactly how much will depend on how much you leave and how many other surviving close relatives you have).

If you die intestate *after* the divorce is finalised, your spouse will have no automatic right to any of your estate. (Your children would probably inherit the estate). However, provided he or she has not remarried, he or she can make a special application to the court for a share of your estate on the basis that you should have provided for his or her maintenance after your death. If the court thinks it would have been reasonable for you to make such provision, it can order provision to be made for your spouse out of your estate.

2. If you have a will
If you die after decree *absolute* of divorce has been granted

leaving a will made before you were divorced, then unless you have made it clear in your will that you intend your former spouse's position under it to be unaffected by the divorce, any gift you have made to him therein will automatically become ineffective, as will any appointment of him as your executor. On the other hand, if you die before decree absolute (even if decree *nisi* of divorce has been granted), your spouse will still be able to benefit from any gift to him in your will. It is therefore advisable to make a fresh will catering for your new circumstances to ensure that your property will pass to whoever you wish to inherit it. However, whatever you do, you cannot rule out absolutely the possibility that your spouse may make an application for provision out of your estate for his or her maintenance just as he or she could have done, had you died intestate.

27
Further Help and Information

There are numerous other books and leaflets available which may be of interest to you on divorce and related topics, and a considerable number of organisations to which you may like to turn for help and support. This chapter lists only a few suggestions.

Publications

You will no doubt have come across relevant pamphlets and leaflets yourself. The Lord Chancellor's Office produces an excellent free guide to divorce procedure for anyone acting without a solicitor. It is called 'Undefended divorce – A guide for the petitioner acting without a solicitor' and is available at the offices of the divorce county court. If you are contemplating dealing with the divorce itself on your own, without a solicitor, this guide may give you all the information you need (provided your case is relatively straightforward). It would be useful reading for those who do have a solicitor as well.

Other official leaflets are available on various topics, for example, legal aid, social security benefits, rent and rate rebates.

The sources of these leaflets are mentioned whenever the leaflets are referred to in the text of this book. The Citizens' Advice Bureaux are generally a good source of supply for information of this kind. The Inland Revenue produce a brief guide to the income tax implications of a marriage breakdown. The present issue is called 'Separation and Divorce' and is also referred to as leaflet IR30. While the leaflet offers guidance it is not the law and opinions of the Revenue given in it do not affect your right of appeal in any tax dispute. The local office of the Inland Revenue can supply the leaflet.

If you want to get hold of further books on divorce and related matters, you should ask a good bookseller or your public library.

Organisations

Some organisations are local, some have branches nationwide. All tend to vary in their standards of efficiency and helpfulness depending on the individuals in charge in the particular area. At best, organisations can be friendly, informative and supportive and of course, at worst, can turn out to be opinionated and cranky. It is really up to you to seek out the organisations most suited to your needs by trial and error and recommendation from friends.

One well-known organisation is the National Marriage Guidance Council. They provide skilled professional help from counsellors specially trained to help when a marriage is going wrong. You will find them in the telephone book. If you want help, simply ring and make an appointment. They will not tell you what to do – they will help you to decide what is best for you and, if you decide you will have to separate, they will help you to do so as painlessly as possible. The Council also publishes a range of booklets on family matters. You can obtain further information by writing to:

The National Marriage Guidance Council,
Herbert Gray College,
Little Church Street,
Rugby,
Warwickshire. CV21 3AP

The National Council for One Parent Families exists to improve the position of single parents and their children. It offers personal help and advice to parents on their own (in the London area), answers telephone and written enquiries and provides written information. Its information office produces up-to-date leaflets and information sheets on a variety of topics. For further information on the services the organisation can offer, write sending a stamped addressed envelope to:

The Information Office,
One Parent Families,
255 Kentish Town Road,
London, NW5 2LX.

Gingerbread is another organisation for one parent families you may have heard of – probably with a branch in your 'phone book.

The Samaritans – should you feel suicidal or lost in despair through the breakdown of your marriage – will always welcome your call – day or night – see your local 'phone directory.

If you wish to get in touch with a local organisation that will help you with your particular needs, it is a good idea to ask your local Citizens' Advice Bureau for some addresses and contacts. They should have on file most of the organisations that have branches operating in your area. Since there can be many different factors involved in a marriage breakdown perhaps connected with extreme difficulties being faced by one or other of you, or even another member of the family, knowledge of where to seek help can be invaluable. Alcohol Concern, MIND, NACRO, NAVH and SCODA (National Association for Mental Health, National Association for the Care and Resettlement of Offenders, National Association of Voluntary Hostels, Standing Conference on Drug Abuse) are some very useful organisations which you could find out more about from your local CAB or through a local Social Worker.

Do not forget that relatives and friends, your clergyman, your doctor, etc., may also be able to help you over difficulties that arise.

INDEX

OTHER GREAT PAPERFRONT BOOKS

Each uniform with this book

WRITE YOUR OWN WILL

Keith Best's book contains all you need to make a proper legal Will yourself. Sample Wills designed to cover most circumstances are included in the book. If you are wealthy, or your affairs are complicated, then you should consult a solicitor about your Will after reading this book, which will guide you as to the questions you should ask.

WHAT TO DO WHEN SOMEONE HAS DEBT PROBLEMS

John McQueen shows you how to move fast and objectively, to delay the claims against you and guide you back to solvency. The legal realities are explained through case histories and experiences of the hundreds of people he has helped since he founded the Association of Bankrupts.

BUYING OR SELLING A HOUSE

Written by Michael Llewelyn, estate agent and a Fellow of the Royal Institution of Chartered Surveyors, this book gives comprehensive coverage of the legal and financial pitfalls which beset the home buyer or seller. Covers mortgages, surveys, solicitors and how to sell without an estate agent.

THE RIGHT WAY TO APPLY FOR A JOB

Whether you have had to move house and lost your job, or if you want to take up part-time or full-time work after a period out of the labour market, Arthur Wilcox gives you all the advice you need.

PAPERFRONT COOKBOOKS

Each uniform with this book

HOW TO BOIL AN EGG

A marvellous book for anyone suddenly faced with having to cook for themselves. Jan Arkless gives hundreds of simple recipes and hints for quick, economical meals and snacks for one. She covers the cooking of vegetables, meats, fish, rice, pasta and so on, and, of course, how to boil an egg!

MICROWAVE COOKING PROPERLY EXPLAINED

Annette Yates explains simply and clearly how a microwave oven works and helps you choose the best equipment. Written for both present and prospective microwave owners, it shows how the versatile microwave oven can transform life for the busy cook.

The book includes a wide selection of over 90 recipes, devised and tested by Annette Yates, each of which has also obtained the seal of approval from her family and friends.

OUT OF THE FREEZER INTO THE MICROWAVE

In this book Annette Yates concentrates on how to make the best *combined* use of your freezer and microwave to save time and effort as never before. You can banish hours of kitchen-slavery yet still produce mouth-watering meals for yourself, family and friends.

The book is packed with 54 additional easy, family-size recipes, each of which carries specific instructions in a unique layout which shows freezer life, cooking times and defrosting times, as well as the times for reheating.

ELLIOT RIGHT WAY BOOKS
KINGSWOOD, SURREY, U.K.

OUR PUBLISHING POLICY

HOW WE CHOOSE

Our policy is to consider every deserving manuscript and we can give special editorial help where an author is an authority on his subject but an inexperienced writer. We are rigorously selective in the choice of books we publish. We set the highest standards of editorial quality and accuracy. This means that a *Paperfront* is easy to understand and delightful to read. Where illustrations are necessary to convey points of detail, these are drawn up by a subject specialist artist from our panel.

HOW WE KEEP PRICES LOW

We aim for the big seller. This enables us to order enormous print runs and achieve the lowest price for you. Unfortunately, this means that you will not find in the *Paperfront* list any titles on obscure subjects of minority interest only. These could not be printed in large enough quantities to be sold for the low price at which we offer this series.

We sell almost all our *Paperfronts* at the same unit price. This saves a lot of fiddling about in our clerical departments and helps us to give you world-beating value. Under this system, the longer titles are offered at a price which we believe to be unmatched by any publisher in the world.

OUR DISTRIBUTION SYSTEM

Because of the competitive price, and the rapid turnover, *Paperfronts* are possibly the most profitable line a bookseller can handle. They are stocked by the best bookshops all over the world. It may be that your bookseller has run out of stock of a particular title. If so, he can order more from us at any time—we have a fine reputation for "same day" despatch, and we supply any order, however small (even a single copy), to any bookseller who has an account with us. We prefer you to buy from your bookseller, as this reminds him of the strong underlying public demand for *Paperfronts*. Members of the public who live in remote places, or who are housebound, or whose local bookseller is uncooperative, can order direct from us by post.

FREE

If you would like an up-to-date list of all Paperfront titles currently available, send a stamped self-addressed envelope to
ELLIOT RIGHT WAY BOOKS, BRIGHTON RD.,
LOWER KINGSWOOD SURREY U.K